Writing to Reason

For My Parents

Writing to Reason:

A Companion for Philosophy Students and Instructors

Brian David Mogck

Blackwell
Publishing

BLACKWELL PUBLISHING
350 Main Street, Malden, MA 02148-5020, USA
9600 Garsington Road, Oxford OX4 2DQ, UK
550 Swanston Street, Carlton, Victoria 3053, Australia

First published 2008 by Blackwell Publishing Ltd

1   2008

Library of Congress Cataloging-in-Publication Data

Mogck, Brian David.
   Writing to reason : a companion for philosophy students and instructors / Brian David
Mogck.
       p. cm.
   Includes bibliographical references and index.
   ISBN 978-1-4051-7099-4 (pbk. : alk. paper)
1. Philosophy—Authorship.   I. Title.

   B52.7.M64 2008
   808′.0661—dc22

                                 2007018631

A catalogue record for this title is available from the British Library.

Set in 10.5/13pt Galliard
by SNP Best-set Typesetter Ltd., Hong Kong

The publisher's policy is to use permanent paper from mills that operate a sustainable
forestry policy, and which has been manufactured from pulp processed using acid-free and
elementary chlorine-free practices. Furthermore, the publisher ensures that the text paper
and cover board used have met acceptable environmental accreditation standards.

For further information on
Blackwell Publishing, visit our website at
www.blackwellpublishing.com

Contents

Preface: A Users' Guide

P.1 A Note to Instructors

P.1.1 Genesis of this companion

I began to compose this companion after grading a stack of midterm papers two feet tall. I noticed that I was making mostly the same comments on each student's paper. It seemed more economical to write the comments once, and refer the students to the master copy of comments as needed.

If an instructor is grading hundreds of papers, it is often impossible to continue writing detailed criticisms and explanations of mistakes pertaining to the composition of an essay, while remaining engaged with its philosophical content. Consequently, instructors' comments might tend to become less detailed or thorough by the hundredth paper. And the comments that are made can become impatient in tone and cryptic in content. Neither is constructive. Using this companion to address the most common problems students have with philosophical composition will facilitate more substantive, philosophical engagement between instructors and their students.

P.1.2 The utility of explicit standards for evaluation

This companion is different from other guides to writing philosophy papers in that it is written with the express purpose of facilitating communication between instructors and students about the criteria that instructors use to evaluate written work.

First, students who read this companion will know what a philosophy paper is supposed to accomplish, how philosophers expect that aim to be achieved, and what are some of the most common reasons that papers fail to realize their purpose. It is important for students to know from the outset that their instructors use relatively objective criteria to evaluate papers, even if philosophers do not generally deal in precisely-quantifiable data. If students are to appreciate the excitement and importance of the humanities, then they have to have some sense of what constitutes success in those domains.

Second, instructors will have an efficient way to refer students to detailed explanations of instructions, advice, and criticism that the instructor is unlikely to write out repeatedly. It is important that instructors not only communicate their expectations before having students submit their written work – something that is accomplished by making this companion available – but also provide some indication of the rationale for those expectations and some directions for meeting them. Using this companion will help instructors to communicate the basics of philosophical writing to all of their students, while permitting them to focus primarily on orchestrating philosophical dialogue with and among their students.

P.1.3 How to use this companion in grading papers

Probably the most common deficiency in undergraduate philosophy papers is the lack of a clear thesis that is defended by cogent reasoning. The instructor's problem in grading, however, is that students cannot always recognize initially the lack of a thesis or cogent reasoning. Depending on the quality of their secondary schooling, they might not even know what a thesis is or what counts as cogent reasoning. So, writing "Where's your thesis?" in the margin might not accomplish anything. I further assume there are no instructors with schedules so luxurious that they have time to sit down and explain to each student individually, for every assignment, what it would have taken to formulate a thesis and argue for it in that particular paper.

Using this companion is one means of explaining to students what philosophy instructors want, why they want it, and how to tell whether a paper has it. If this companion is used, an instructor who encounters a paper without a thesis may still write "Thesis" in the margin. But the instructor will be referring the student to the detailed discussion in *ℓ* 5 of what a thesis is, why a philosophy paper needs one, and how to formulate one.

P.1.4 This companion can facilitate, but cannot substitute for the unique insights of instructors

Obviously, this companion cannot substitute for the unique insights into philosophy and philosophical writing that each instructor brings to his or her classes. This companion is intended as a supplement and a reference point. But, it is to be expected that instructors will teach their students about writing papers by supplementing or improving upon the guidance offered herein.

Chapter 8 sets forth one view of *doing philosophy* that is intended only to orient students to the discipline. It is more difficult and controversial than the rest of the companion, and for this reason I would like to alert instructors that they may or may not wish to assign it, depending on whether they think that what I have said compliments the philosophical and pedagogical values they intend to cultivate in their courses. I remind students in several places that the view of philosophy offered there is only intended to get them started thinking about what *they* think philosophy is – an enterprise that will be primarily stimulated and guided by their instructors and the texts of their courses. Part I is the practical interface that is designed to make grading more efficient for instructors, and may be used independently of Part II.

P.1.5 Is this companion a grading rubric?

A "grading rubric" consists of: (a) a set of standards that are used in grading; and (b) some explanation of the degrees of success in achieving them (for example, poor, good, excellent, etc.). Sometimes, these standards are presented in a chart with the standards running along one axis and classifications of success along the other. Maralee Harrell has described a rubric that she uses in which the main categories of evaluation are Content and Style (Harrell 2005). The subcategories of Content include Argument, Understanding, Analysis, Synthesis, and Creation. The subcategories of Style include Clarity and Organization. She constructs a grading grid – that is, a chart setting out the (sub)categories and levels of achievement – and assigns points to each box of the grid (e.g., "Good" for "Thesis" earns the student 4 points out of 85 total).

This companion might be thought of as a grading rubric insofar as it sets out the standards of success in philosophical writing. However, I have not offered below a systematic description of the degrees of success in meeting these standards. The reason for this is that which standards apply to which types of assignments in which classes and (most importantly) what is the relative weight attached to the degrees of meeting these standards will be different for almost any two assignments a teacher makes (Harrell 2005: 4–5). This companion, however, is intended to have wider application than any course- or assignment-specific rubric.

Nonetheless, if teachers who plan to use this companion also plan to use a rubric or a grading grid, this companion will be a welcome companion piece. It explains the principles according to which philosophers tend to measure success in the field, and endeavors to communicate the attitude that philosophers tend to take towards their work.

P.2 A Note to Students

P.2.1 Beginning students

This companion for writing philosophy papers was written primarily for undergraduates, especially those who may be writing a philosophy paper for the first time, or who just want a better grasp of what their instructors expect.

P.2.2 Advanced students

Advanced undergraduates and graduate students will also find more than a few areas covered in this companion in which they can improve. I benefited from reviewing its contents while I was writing my doctoral dissertation. And had I paid better attention to the lessons in this companion, there would have been fewer confusing explanations and obscure inferences than there were! Because many of these lessons are fundamental, they bear repeating, even to experienced writers.

P.2.3 Philosophy majors

Third- or fourth-year Philosophy majors should have already received individualized writing instruction from an advisor or another instructor under whose direction they have studied. For any advanced student who has not yet received such individualized instruction, I recommend that you:

1 pick your two best writing samples that are under 10 pages (double spaced, 12-point font);
2 ask the instructor you consider to be the best scholar in your department (not necessarily the one you think is the friendliest) to read them;
3 tell him or her that you want to devise a plan to improve your writing; and
4 ask for a 20 minute appointment to get his or her advice.

This sort of conversation will likely provide you with valuable feedback not only on the way you write, but also on the way you tend to approach philosophical texts and problems.

P.2.4 How to use this companion

This is a relatively short companion. But it contains a number of instructions that you will not be able to internalize immediately. After all, writing is a craft that improves only with disciplined practice. And, even if this companion is successful, it only covers some of the most common characteristics of good writing in philosophy.

Students sometimes find that they are asked to write a philosophy paper without first having an idea of what it means to do philosophy or how philosophical writing differs from writing in other disciplines. Part II explains one view of what it means to do philosophy, how to succeed in a philosophy course, how to approach a philosophy paper, and the requirements of academic integrity. Chapter 8 is the most difficult and controversial chapter of this companion, because it is an account of what philosophers are doing when they are *doing philosophy*. This is neither easy to explain nor likely to elicit much agreement among philosophers. For this reason, your instructor may or may not recommend that you read it, depending on his or her judgment as to whether that view fits well with his or her goals for the course. That is just fine, as Part I is the practical part of the companion.

In order to use Part I effectively, I would recommend that you first look it over to identify those points that you are encountering for the first time and those points that you suspect are problematic in your own writing. Later, as you compose your paper and work through the drafting process, you can refer back to those points and check them off to make sure that you have addressed them. (Other checklists can be found in sections 1.1, 1.4, and 1.6).

Your instructor will also refer you in either of two ways to specific parts of the companion. First, he or she might write a numeral in the margin of your paper – for example, "5" – indicating that there is a problem in your paper that is addressed in ℓ 5 of this book. Second, he or she might highlight a theme that is problematic in the essay – for example, the thesis is unclear – by writing the keyword "Thesis" on your paper. You may then look up the keyword in the *Keywords Cross-referenced* table (see Appendix I) to find the sections of this companion that contain specific commentary and advice addressing that issue.

P.2.5 A note recommending writing centers

Most high schools do not adequately prepare their students to write college-level expository papers. Undergraduates often do not receive the instruction and practice they need to improve their writing significantly. Especially if classes are large, instructors might not have time to read drafts of papers. Nevertheless, two things are certain: (a) you will not catch all of your own mistakes; a second pair of eyes will help; and, (b) under no circumstances should the first draft of your paper be submitted for a grade. Some schools have writing centers where students can receive help editing and revising from experienced writers. Students should consider visiting a writing center or otherwise consulting successful writers for needed advice and encouragement.

P.2.6 Keep records of any special instructions

Do not throw away written instructions or delete electronic messages that contain special instructions about an assignment until the course is over and you know you will not be appealing your grade. Also, be sure to save a record of any communication from the instructor that gives you an extension or alters the instructions or expectations for an assignment. Instructors sometimes forget that they gave a student an extension or indicated that they would accept a different format, topic, or approach than what was originally assigned. Unless you have documentary evidence *authored by the instructor* to verify your position, the instructor probably will not take your word that you are the one person in the class who does not have to follow the rules. If you originally received oral permission to deviate from one of the original requirements, then send an email confirming the exemption and ask for a confirming response.

P.2.7 Are the criteria of evaluation in philosophy subjective or objective?

Some people think that because philosophers do not always give multiple choice exams or ask questions that have provable answers (except, of course, in logic classes) that grading philosophy papers is somehow more *subjective* than grading a chemistry experiment. However, when you write a philosophy paper, you will probably make claims about, for example, what is the conclusion of a philosopher's argument, whether a philosopher relied upon a certain premise in constructing his or her argument, whether an argument is valid, whether certain premises are true or whether one philosopher agrees or disagrees with or was influenced by another philosopher. All of these issues are matters of objective fact in the same way that $2 + 2 = 4$ and Lisbon is the capital of Portugal are both objective facts. If you make the sort of claim that is either true or false (e.g., "The Stoic Chrysippus accepted Socrates' view that virtue is a form of knowledge") and what you claim is false, then the flaw in your paper is *objective*, not subjective.[1]

---

[1] Note, however, that from the observation that a claim is either true or false as a matter of objective fact, it does not follow that everyone – even all those who know something about Chrysippus and Socrates and Hellenistic philosophy – necessarily agrees on the answer. It does tell us something important about the valid grounds for asserting or criticizing such a claim: such a claim stands or falls depending on the textual and historical *evidence*. The fact that philosophy papers contain many factual assertions was emphasized to me by Coleen Zoller. The fact that philosophers sometimes disagree even on factual assertions was emphasized to me by an anonymous reviewer.

Furthermore, grading a philosophy paper requires that a human being actually reads it, rather than feeds a bubble sheet through a Scantron™ machine (as with many standardized tests). In this very trivial and obvious sense, there is an unavoidable subjective element in grading a philosophy paper, because a human subject processes the information and assigns a score. But this is true in chemistry class too, given that a human being has to read the section of your lab report in which you analyze the data in order to determine to what extent you have understood the underlying reactions. And it is true in math class when a human being decides how much partial credit you deserve for an imperfect proof. Insofar as they are making judgments by applying criteria to evaluate your work, there is not a significant difference in how your instructors from different departments assign grades.

The important question is not whether instructors exercise their scholarly judgment in assigning grades, but whether the criteria that are applied in those judgments are objective *in the following senses*:

☑ Do the criteria pertain to observable properties of the paper rather than the idiosyncratic feelings of the grader?
☑ Are the criteria made public so that students can know in advance what they are expected to accomplish?
☑ Are the criteria stable once they have been publicized or are they a moving target?

In order to improve your writing, you have to know what needs improvement. And if the standards are too idiosyncratic to a grader, if they are not known ahead of time, if they change from one assignment to the next, or if their application is inconsistent, then you will not learn anything useful from the instructor's evaluation. These concerns are met by using this companion as an interface between the instructor and student to coordinate expectations.

Part of learning a new discipline is learning what counts as success among the participants. One way to begin learning what counts as success in the discipline of philosophy is to read this companion. Another way is to watch your instructor model philosophical expression in classroom lectures and discussions. A third way is to read excellent philosophical writing in journals and books. Probably you will do all three. As you participate in the discipline, you will become conscious of certain consistent themes that indicate what must be done in order to do philosophy well.

Acknowledgments

Many of the insights expressed in this companion were imparted to me by my teachers at Hamline University and Emory University. I would especially like to acknowledge the lasting impact that Professor Nancy Holland and Professor Steven Kellert of Hamline University have had on my view of philosophy and philosophical writing. Of course, I alone am responsible for the views set out below. But I do hope to have honored their influence. I am also grateful to Professor Coleen Zoller, Jeff Dean of Blackwell, and the anonymous reviewers of the manuscript for many insightful suggestions on earlier versions of this book.

Glossary of Philosophical Terms

What follows is a glossary of philosophical terms that are used at various places in this book. It is included so that beginning students will not encounter a terminological barrier to the explanations that follow and so that advanced students and instructors know what I mean on those few occasions when I use philosophical jargon.

Perhaps the main purpose of providing a glossary is to alert students to the fact that all of the terms that follow are *terms of art* – that is, specifically defined terms that are typically used precisely and technically. And philosophers usually think that there are important distinctions between these terms – between "proposition" and "sentence," for example. Thus, you will do well to attend to the meaning of these terms especially, when you read and write philosophy.

There is no such thing as an uncontroversial, widely-accepted glossary of philosophical terminology. So please take the "definitions" that follow as provisional, to be used only to orient you within the vocabulary that philosophers routinely employ. All I mean to indicate by providing "definitions" is: *philosophers often use these terms to mean something like this* . . . Even dictionaries and encyclopedias of philosophy tend only to provide a critical overview of the main uses of philosophical terminology.

Some terms are explained in detail elsewhere in this companion – especially terms pertaining to arguments – so I do not include them

here. Some of the terms that are included below will be further expli-
cated in the companion when they are at issue.[2]

Assertion	A person makes an *assertion* when he or she uses a sentence in order to state a proposition. An *assertion* is a type of utterance.
Belief	*Belief* is cognitive assent; that is, it is the attitude of accepting or endorsing a proposition as true.
Concept	Philosophers used to think of concepts as mental pictures of things, but maybe they will turn out to be patterns of neurons in our brains. *Concepts* are the basic building blocks of thought. One has a concept of *dog*, and of *Retriever*, but a thought *that the dog is a Retriever*.
Conceptual competence	A person demonstrates *conceptual competence* if she behaves in a way that shows that she is able to use a concept correctly. A person who states that the number six is green clearly lacks conceptual competence with respect to either the concept "green," the concept "six," or both.
Epistemology	*Epistemology* is the study of knowledge. Psychology and cognitive science are important parts of epistemology, which aim to explain reliable perception, the formation of correct beliefs, and competent behavior. There is usually thought to be an important normative component of a theory of knowledge; namely, the conditions under which a person is *justified* or *warranted* in holding a belief.

---

[2] I am grateful to one of the anonymous reviewers for Blackwell, who provided
important criticisms and suggestions for the glossary, especially for the entries
pertaining to language and mind.

Ethics

Ethics is the study of virtue, duty, human well-being, and, generally, whatever bears on the evaluation of human action (including its motivations and consequences) as right or wrong. Philosophers tend to use "ethical" and "moral" interchangeably; so, for example, "ethical responsibility" and "moral responsibility" generally refer to the same thing.

Inquiry

Inquiry is the problem-solving use of human intelligence. It is characterized by open-mindedness, free participation, lively discussion, vigorous criticism, experimentation, observation, and analysis.

Intersubjective

The basic meaning of *intersubjective* is *between individuals.* In philosophical contexts, the term "intersubjective" also indicates that individuals might collaborate, coordinate, or agree on something as a matter of social fact or practical need. "Intersubjective" is perhaps best contrasted with the term "unilateral" or "private," rather than the more obvious alternative "subjective."

Justification

Justification is a property a person has if he or she is right to believe or do something. A person might be justified in believing a proposition if he or she formed the belief through a reliable process or the person has good reasons for believing it or the person believes it based on good authority. A "justified belief" is a belief a person is justified in holding.

Knowledge

Defining *knowledge* is the task of the branch of philosophy called *epistemology.* The most commonly-glossed definition of knowledge is: a *belief* that one is *justified* in holding and that is *true.*

Language   The term *language* in philosophy may refer either to a *formal* or a *natural* language. English and Parsi are natural languages. A formal language is the sort of thing that mathematical logicians and some linguists study. A formal language consists of symbols (such as names) and rules for combining those symbols to form sentences (rules of syntax). A formal language is the complete set of all "grammatical" sentences that can be formed from the stock of symbols. Formal languages are generally constructed to model some (part of) natural language.

Logic   *Logic* is the study of correct reasoning. It is closely related to the field of semantics (see below).

Logical consequence   The standard definition of *logical consequence* (slightly simplified) is that one sentence – call it "C" – is a logical consequence of another sentence – call it "P" – if and only if C must be true whenever P is true. We then say that C *logically follows* from P.

Metaphysics   *Metaphysics* is the study of reality. It is thus broader than the study of nature (what we usually call *science*) and narrower than the study of existence (what we usually call *ontology*).

Normative   Something is *normative* if it pertains to the rules that govern what is right. Normative terms such as *good/bad, justified/unjustified, rational/irrational*, etc. are evaluative terms, indicating success or failure in meeting certain standards.

Objective   *Objective* is generally used in philosophy to describe things (usually properties or facts) that are mind-independent. *Objec-*

tive is usually contrasted with *subjective*. What it takes for facts, values or inquiry to be objective is a matter of heated controversy. One usage that attempts to remain noncommittal on the underlying metaphysical questions holds that something is *objective* insofar as it is public, amenable to empirical and/or experimental testing, and rationally responsive to criticism.

Ontology
Ontology is the study of what exists or, perhaps better, what it means to say of something that it exists (or does not). One important question in ontology is, "What sorts of objects must exist in order for a theory to be true?"

Proposition
A proposition is what is expressed by a sentence. Some think that propositions are the sorts of things that can be true or false, and that a true sentence is just a sentence that expresses a true proposition. Propositions, like thoughts, depict possible states-of-affairs. Different sentences in different languages may express the same proposition: "Snow is white" in English, "*La neige est blanche*" in French, and "*Schnee ist weiß*" in German all express the proposition *that snow is white*.

Rationality
Rationality is the capacity to approach problems with the primary objective of having adequate justification for a course of action or manner of thought. One's exercise of rationality typically involves correct reasoning (that is, logical argument) and publicly-available evidence (of which empirical evidence is the best example). A person's behavior or thought is rational if it is the result of the successful exercise of rationality.

Semantics
Semantics is the study of how meaning attaches to words and sentences, in which the truth-conditions of a sentence and the logical relations among sentences generally play an important role. The term "semantic" is often used in a pejorative sense in American English. "Arguing semantics" is an accusation one makes if the other person is quibbling over words, rather than addressing what is really at stake. "Semantic" in philosophy and logic means something completely different.

Sentence
Sentences are grammatically correct strings of words. Sentences pertaining to how things stand in the world are linguistic expressions of propositions. There are plenty of other types of sentences – such as "I promise . . ." for example – but philosophers are usually interested in the ones that state facts – declarative sentences.

Statement
A *statement* is a sentence that is expressed.

Subjective
Subjective is contrasted with *objective* and designates things (usually facts or properties) that exist in virtue of the state of someone's mind. Usually philosophers talk about experiences (especially perceptions) and thoughts as being *subjective*. Alternatively, *subjectivity* generally refers either to an individual's status *as a subject* – in the sense of an individual who is capable of action and responsibility, also called an "agent" – or to an individual's experience of things that are subjective, which some philosophers simply refer to as "consciousness."

Thought
Usually we talk about thoughts *of something* or thoughts *that something is the case.*

Thoughts, like propositions, depict possible states-of-affairs: *that a cat is on a mat*, for example. Maybe thoughts and propositions are the same thing, but thoughts are generally thought to be mental and propositions linguistic. Thus, if there exists even one thought that cannot adequately be put into language (*any* language), then thoughts and propositions are not the same thing.

Truth One of the most controversial terms in philosophy, *truth* is a property of a sentence just in case (to mention a few options): (a) the sentence states a fact; (b) there is a proof of the sentence; or (c) the sentence expresses a proposition that is a correct picture of, or otherwise adequate to, some part of the world.

Truth conditions The *truth conditions* of a sentence are the states of affairs that must hold in the world for a sentence to be true. The truth conditions of the sentence "Snow is white" are simply that crystals of frozen H_2O must reflect all wavelengths of light equally.

Utterance An *utterance* is an oral, written, or gestural expression of a sentence.

Warrant A person who believes a true proposition is not usually thought to know the proposition, unless he or she believes it for the right reasons or formed the belief in the right way. The normative element referred to by "the right reasons" and "the right way" is also referred to as the *warrant* a person has for believing a true proposition if he or she knows it. Many philosophers do not distinguish between *justification* and *warrant* (recall that knowledge was glossed above as *justified, true belief*), but some do.

Word   Just as concepts are the constituents of thoughts, so *words* are the constituents of sentences. Most of our concepts can be named by words, but probably not all of them. And some words might not have concepts associated with them – "Yippie!" for example.

Part I

Writing Philosophy

1

Writing a Philosophy Paper

1.1 What is a Philosophy Paper Supposed to Accomplish?

The point of writing a philosophy paper is to demonstrate in writing that you have thought carefully about the issues presented in the texts you have read and to make an argument pertaining to one of these issues. The paper will be better the more carefully you have:

- ☑ read and re-read the texts;
- ☑ thought through the claims made by the author;
- ☑ thought through the arguments offered for these claims;
- ☑ thought through the argument you want to make in your paper; and
- ☑ crafted your paper so that your writing facilitates the expression of thoughts, as opposed to obscuring them.

Your task is to write a paper that:

- ☑ has a clearly-stated thesis and a clearly-defined structure;
- ☑ makes an interesting argument or develops an accurate interpretation of a text;
- ☑ is supported by adequate and appropriate quotations;
- ☑ explains the meaning of the quotations and the significance of the quotations to your argument, and
- ☑ contains no grammatical or typographical errors.

An instructor's evaluation of a paper usually focuses on these requirements.

1.2 Choosing a Topic

Philosophy instructors often allow students to choose the topics of their papers. This may not strike every student with equal glee, for not every student is equally taken with the class or the readings. That is fine. Philosophy is difficult and often obscure, and one does not need to do philosophy to be a rational and reflective person.[1] It may strike others with vertigo if they find the class and the readings particularly fascinating. These students run the risk of picking a topic that is too ambitious for the assignment. So let me offer separate advice for these two categories of students.

1.2.1 Students who have not found a fascinating topic

First, students who are having difficulty finding something interesting to write about are well-advised to ask their instructor for a suggestion. Instructors often ask students what their interests are outside of philosophy. This information helps the instructors to think of topics that will resonate with their students' chosen areas of study. If your philosophy instructor does not suggest anything that moves you, try asking someone from the department in which you plan to major for topics that would be of interest to them if they were taking your philosophy course.

You might be unable to find a thrilling topic, in which case you will have to settle for a topic that simply makes for a good paper. Here, it helps to have paid attention in class, because instructors often tell you what *they* find most interesting or confusing in the texts you are reading. Sometimes they even say during a lecture: "It would make for a good paper if you could make sense out of such-and-such." If nothing suggestive has been said in class, try asking the instructor to suggest a question that would be worthy of appearing on a final exam. Such a question will present a problem that the instructor thinks is difficult and interesting. If you address such a question in your paper, you have a good opportunity to demonstrate your understanding of the texts and the underlying concepts and arguments.

---

[1] Philosophy as an academic discipline does not have a monopoly in the marketplace of ideas, even if it exercises considerable market power in setting the terms and the standards for many debates and oftentimes offers a superior product.

If all else fails, try approaching an especially sharp colleague in the class, convey your predicament, and ask for ideas. Maybe your colleague considered writing on topics A and B, but decided finally to write on topic A. You may be able to write on your colleague's plan B if three conditions are met: first you must ask for permission to use it (as he or she may have planned to use the idea for a different paper); second, if permission is granted, you must acknowledge in a footnote somewhere at the beginning of the paper that your able colleague Ms. So-And-So kindly suggested the topic; third, you must only use the *topic* – which could be stated in one relatively general sentence – and not any arguments, research, or writing that are not your own original contribution. If the source is acknowledged, borrowing an idea is not plagiarism. But the expression and development of the idea must be altogether your own.[2] If these three conditions are satisfied, the paper meets the criteria for responsible and original academic work. Nevertheless, it is wise first to get approval for your plan before you begin to carry it out, as policies may vary across instructors and schools.

1.2.2 Students who have found a fascinating topic

Students who already think that philosophy is the most interesting thing you could possibly spend your time doing also have difficulty, not in generating ideas, but in focusing on one that will make for a good paper. Papers usually have to be written under certain constraints. You will only have a certain number of days until it is due. You might only have a certain number of pages or words in which to develop your argument. A good topic for a ten page paper may be a disastrous topic for a five page paper. And a topic that is well within your intellectual reach given a month of thinking and writing may be quite beyond your competence if given only a few days.

The best way to address the problem of constraints is to identify the argument you want to make and determine what part of it you can develop and defend under the circumstances. The purpose of your paper will be *to defend a certain part of an argument*; it will not be to make the broader, more ambitious argument all in one go. In

---

[2] See Chapter 6 for further explanation of plagiarism and how to avoid it.

choosing which part of the argument to explicate, consider tackling the most problematic aspect of the broader argument. Focus on the premise or inference in your broader argument that your reader will probably have the most trouble accepting. Explain the broader argument and how this discrete part fits into it. Tell the reader what you intend to accomplish, so he or she knows what to expect from your work.

It is common for an author to state that certain relevant issues and arguments cannot be addressed, because they are "outside the scope of the present paper." This is often a legitimate excuse. But you should not open a can of worms and then tell the reader that dealing with it is outside the scope of your paper. You may decline to treat certain *relevant* issues. However, you will have to explain certain concepts and defend certain inferences in order for your thesis to make any sense or have the slightest plausibility. You may not sweep such essential components of your present argument under the rug.

1.2.3 Supplemental reading ought not to become the primary focus of your paper

Enthusiastic students often do extra reading. This is often an edifying and productive practice, but there are also risks. The first is having your attention prematurely focused on one aspect of a text before you have a good grasp of the text as a whole. The second is picking up technical jargon that it may only be appropriate for professionals to use.[3]

Students who want to be aided but not distracted by extra reading might do well not to take notes on the supplemental text and not to look at that text while writing their papers. If you take notes, it is too easy to think of those notes as something important that has to be incorporated somehow into your paper. But that is not true, given

---

[3] Of course, learning the jargon is one step in becoming a member of a discipline. But first we read the texts, learn the arguments, learn the historical context of the debate, and only afterwards do we acquire the privilege of using verbal shorthand. It is almost always better to offer an explanation than to use a fancy term. For further discussion of using what I call five-star vocabulary words, see ℓ 25.

that your extra reading should only enrich your reading and under-standing of the arguments in the primary text. It is, of course, appro-priate to acknowledge in your paper where a secondary source has helped you to think through your own argument.[4]

1.2.4 On better and worse targets for philosophical analysis

It is important when choosing a topic for philosophical analysis to focus on a target that is amenable to critical scrutiny with respect to its argument and the concepts employed. It would be an exceedingly strange project (for the purposes of most academic papers) to subject a love note, for example, to philosophical analysis. Now, there is a subfield of philosophy that studies sex and love, so maybe there is a place for it after all. But presumably the author of a love note has no intention of justifying his or her statements or making much literal sense or employing concepts consistently or employing coherent con-cepts at all. Showing that its conclusion (if there is one) does not follow logically from its premises or that the concepts employed are incoherent would be like playing the harpsichord with a jackhammer. Usually, your target text was chosen for you by the instructor when he or she made the assignment. But if you are able to choose your target, I would recommend that you focus on cultural artifacts (for example, books, or theories, or doctrines) that are *supposed to be* ratio-nally defensible.

Students should be careful when they undertake *philosophical* scrutiny of political rhetoric for much the same reasons. Sometimes political rhetoric is not intended to rationally persuade, but rather to arouse passions (for example, by bringing some injustice to the public's attention) or instigate action (for example, by urging the public to address the injustice). In order to become virtuous, one's feelings and dispositions must be trained, in addition to one's intellect; and, for this reason, Aristotle argued in the *Nicomachean Ethics* that politi-cal discourse may legitimately aim to engage one's emotional and

---

[4] For further discussion of the use of secondary sources, see 🖙 45, and for correct attribution, see 🖙 41.

volitional faculties, in addition to one's rational faculty (1984c: II.3.1104b4–1105a17).[5]

Furthermore, Aristotle taught that political and legal rhetoric aims for both rational and affective persuasion: "since rhetoric exists to affect the giving of decisions – the hearers decide between one political speaker and another, and a legal verdict *is* a decision – the orator must not only try to make the argument of his speech demonstrative and worthy of belief; he must also make his own character look right and put his hearers, who are to decide, into the right frame of mind" (1984d: II.1.1377b21–25). That is to say, the orator builds sympathy and confidence at the same time as he or she builds a case.

While a critical attitude is always appropriate when you are confronted with persuasive rhetoric, it will only be edifying to logically scrutinize the cogency of rhetoric that is presented in the form of a reasoned view. This does not mean that the only engagement philosophers have with political rhetoric is evaluating arguments. Philosophers also study the way that concepts, expressed in words or images, are put to use (and, oftentimes, thereby transformed) in order to affect our emotions, actions, or thoughts. However, this sort of project will be more descriptive and phenomenological, rather than formally logical and analytical. This methodological difference is appropriate, for there ought to be some *fit* between the sort of rhetoric you study and the sort of scrutiny to which you subject it. Since philosophical scrutiny is primarily concerned with concepts and arguments – the terms we use to theorize about the world and the justifications we offer to support such theories – you stand a much better chance of writing an interesting philosophy paper if you focus on the philosophical commitments *underlying* political rhetoric and the policies expressed. For the commitments underlying political rhetoric stand a better chance of being rationally articulated and are, thus, more amenable to rational scrutiny.

One common manner of criticizing political rhetoric is to point out contradictions among the reasons offered for certain policies. There

---

[5] Aristotle (384–322 BC) was a member of Plato's Academy, before he served as tutor to Alexander the Great and founded his own school of philosophy. Aristotle's ethics continue to wield great influence. It is fair to say that he invented formal logic and was one of the first natural philosophers whose theories, especially on biology, were informed by extensive observation. Students can expect to read Aristotle in courses on Ancient Philosophy, metaphysics, and ethics. Aristotle is also one of the few philosophers often deemed important enough to warrant an undergraduate course devoted exclusively to his own works.

are three cases to consider. First, if *a policy* is self-contradictory, then we know that it is wrong; for it includes among its commitments two propositions that cannot both be true. Criticism of political rhetoric almost never takes this form, however, because even politicians are usually able to avoid self-contradiction on a single topic, at least in a single breath. Second, if *two policies* are inconsistent, then we know that at least one of them is wrong. If policy A is inconsistent with policy B, then A includes some sentence(s) that cannot be true together with some sentence(s) included in B. This would be the case if, for example, President George W. Bush's policies on terrorism and capital punishment are inconsistent with the sanctity of life ethic that supports his policies on abortion and stem cell research, as Peter Singer (2004) has recently argued.[6] But notice how little we learn if all we know is that two theories cannot both be true together: we know that at least one of the theories is false, but not which one; and, in demonstrating the inconsistency, one does not necessarily explicate the conceptions at stake or evaluate the separate commitments in their own right, which is what primarily interests philosophers. Third, if *one person* expounds two theories that are inconsistent, then, in addition to knowing that the theories cannot both be true together, we have good reason to think that the person is untrustworthy, because the information he or she propounds is corrupt. But do we learn anything about the conceptions or commitments at stake by impugning the source?

The argumentative strategy whereby one shows that one's opponent has contradicted him- or herself is an *argumentum ad homimem* – an argument against the person.[7] Yet, in this case too, there is usually

---

[6]   See especially Chapter 3. I only mention Singer's book as an example of diagnosing inconsistency, not to critique it or recommend it.

[7]   *Ad hominem* arguments are often fallacious. However, they are appropriate in dialectical settings where the credibility of a person figures among the reasons others have to accept his or her statements as likely true. Consider the example of an attorney arguing that the testimony of an expert witness should be excluded from trial because the expert testified to an inconsistent thesis in a different trial one month before. This argument does not show that the expert's current testimony is false, only that the court has reason to view the expert as an unreliable witness whose testimony might serve as an unstable basis for the jury's findings of fact. Since it is a precondition of testifying at all that the expert's testimony be deemed reliable and that the expert witness be deemed trustworthy, offering an *ad hominem* argument for exclusion of the expert's testimony is cogent. See generally Walton (1998: 280) (vindicating the appropriateness of *ad homimen* arguments, however narrowly circumscribed) and (1998: 220–1) (on attacking inconsistent commitments).

nothing of philosophical interest to be gained from such an argument. Consider an example. Suppose I claim that all humans are mortal and that I am a human, and nonetheless claim that I am immortal. My opponent can point out that I am an idiot, because the conclusion I embrace cannot be true together with the premises I accept. However, showing that I am an idiot does not help my opponent to show which of the statements I made is true and which is false, nor does it explicate any concepts or explain any inferences.

Diagnosing inconsistency is a valuable exercise of critical thinking. It is perhaps the first step in recognizing that an explanation someone has offered is logically or conceptually inadequate and fails to command our rational assent. Notwithstanding the fundamental role of critical thinking in thinking philosophically, *doing* philosophy involves more than logical appraisal. It also requires explanation and development of the relevant concepts, and an effort to justify a better understanding of the pertinent issues.

1.2.5 Papers that *discuss* issues

Papers that set out to *discuss* an issue or a text are already off to a bad start. Consider this: how will you know when you are finished? If the paper has a clear thesis and strategy, then you know that you are finished when you have carried out the final step in your strategy. Discussions are usually concluded when the author (or reader!) gets bored or the author runs out of space.

There are a few omens that signal the rise of a discussion and the fall of an argument. First, if you are explaining Marx's argument for the labor theory of value and you find yourself writing, "Marx *also* thinks that . . . ," stop right there. Why do *other* things that Marx thinks deserve to be discussed in your paper? If these other things are part of, or otherwise illuminate Marx's argument for the labor theory of value, then explaining them may be perfectly germane to your strategy. However, you should resist the temptation to discuss passages of Marx's text or aspects of his philosophy simply because they are important or you happen to understand them or you have something insightful to say about them.

Another omen of waxing discussing and waning argument is: "Marx went on to argue . . ." Again, stop there. Marx probably *went on* to argue a lot of things after making the last argument you have discussed. But how does discussing them advance your thesis? Do not confuse sequential progression in the presentation of a thesis with logical argument for the truth of that thesis. You should discuss all and only those passages of a text that the reader has to understand in the manner you propose in order to be rationally convinced of your thesis. Sometimes this will mean that your argument about a philosopher's theory will be limited to those passages laying out the author's argument for that specific theory. Oftentimes, however, great insight is to be gained from considering how a seemingly-unrelated aspect of a philosopher's thought is, in fact, integral to the workings of the theory that is the primary focus of your paper. So do not be narrow-minded in developing your thesis. But, once you have identified the thesis you will develop and defend, your paper should be narrowly-tailored to that objective.

1.3 Moving through Drafts

If you are having trouble getting started, start writing anyway. Other than exercising and showering, I know of no better cure for writers' block than actually writing. You will inevitably think that whatever you write is garbage, and it may well be. That is fine – throw it all away. The point is to get into the process, to let the creative sparks fly. I usually have to go through at least one disastrous beginning for each paper I write. Think of it as a mental cleansing process: the surface clutter has to be cleared away for the worthwhile expression to emerge. Once you have had an opportunity for catharsis, put away all of your books, even take a walk if you like, and ask yourself: "What do I want to say in this paper?" You are ready to start writing in earnest when you can answer that question in a few simple sentences.

If you write a first draft of a paper without having attentively read and reread the texts or carefully planned out your argument, it would be detrimental to think of your second effort as a second "draft." Especially when a paper is in the early stages of development, it is likely to contain more than one mistake that cannot be adequately remedied without rewriting substantially all of the paper. It might sound inefficient to abandon previous efforts. But rewriting from scratch usually produces a more coherent paper. The biggest waste of effort is trying to salvage pages just because they are already written, only to realize after hours of shuffling passages around that the paper no longer follows a single, clear strategy. You may be surprised at how efficiently you can write a paper once you have figured out your argument.

On the other hand, if you have already solidified your argument in your first draft and only need, for example, to add additional textual support for your interpretation of a text, bolster your premises with additional facts or examples or more carefully express your reasoning, then subsequent drafts will engage in the sort of refining and polishing that is generally associated with a second draft. That is to say, if your first draft qualified as a philosophy paper, then it makes sense to work on a second draft; whereas, if your first draft was actually catharsis, brush-clearing, or brainstorming, then it is the better part of prudence to start from scratch with a clear thesis and a well-honed strategy.

1.4 The Only Outline You Need is a Sketch of the Argument You Plan to Make

The structure of your paper is determined by the argument you intend to make. So an outline of your paper is just an overview of that argument. You can construct such an overview by answering these questions:

- ☑ What is the conclusion you want to demonstrate?
- ☑ What are the premises from which your conclusion follows?
- ☑ How are you going to show that your conclusion follows from those premises?
- ☑ How are you going to show that your premises are true?

Sometimes it is helpful to keep track of the passages from the assigned texts that you think it is necessary to quote and explain. As you do so, keep track of what function the quoted passage will serve in your paper. And bear in mind that a passage does not deserve to be quoted in your paper unless something in your argument depends on its existence or meaning. Even the most profound passage in a book does not deserve to be quoted in your paper unless its explication advances your argument.

1.5 The Cardinal Virtues: Logical Rigor and Clarity of Expression

I heard somewhere that the philosopher John Searle[8] once said, "If you can't express a thought clearly, then you've failed to have one." And while it may be apocryphal, as well as hyperbolic, the gist is that if you cannot express a thought clearly, then *no one else will be able to tell* that you have had one. And since you are writing the paper to demonstrate to the instructor that you have thought carefully about the material and have an interesting contribution to make to the philosophical discussion, he or she will not be able to discern this if you do not write clearly. If you are going to have a shot at being profound, then your reader has to be able to grasp your meaning. Obscurity is its own reward.

It is sometimes difficult to write clearly and logically about philosophy. For example, I wrote a thesis as an undergraduate on the French philosopher Jacques Derrida[9] and the German philosopher and literary critic Walter Benjamin[10] treating a topic in the philosophy of history. These figures are part of the Continental tradition in philosophy, which is notorious for being about as clear as mud. After I gave a draft to one of my thesis committee members, the professor said something like this to me: "I can't understand this. Now, I'm quite familiar with Continental philosophy and teach it in my classes. So, if I can't understand

---

[8] Searle is Mills Professor of Philosophy of Mind and Language at the University of California at Berkeley. His research in recent years has focused on explaining consciousness. He has also contributed to the philosophy of language, specifically a development of ordinary language philosophy called "speech act theory." His publications can be found at his website: <http://ist-socrates.berkeley.edu/~jsearle/>.

[9] Jacques Derrida (1930–2004) was an Algerian-born French philosopher who taught at several French and American universities. He is among the most controversial and obscure recent philosophers and is associated with the philosophy of Heidegger, phenomenology, and "deconstruction." A list of his publications can be found at: <http://www.hydra.umn.edu/derrida/jdind.html>.

[10] Walter Benjamin (1892–1940) was a philosopher and scholar primarily of German literature. He is often associated with the Frankfurt School of Critical Theory, a group of interdisciplinary scholars concerned with the irrational and self-destructive tendencies of modern culture. A list of his works can be found at <http://www.wbenjamin.org/wbrs-biblio.html#I>.

something you write, then the problem is with your expression, not my ability to comprehend it. If the final version of your thesis contains anything that I simply cannot understand, then it will not pass." After I picked myself up off the floor, I rewrote the entire thesis, and thankfully it passed. I have never forgotten this admonition because, although it was sobering, I needed to hear it. And I had to agree with it then, just as I do now. Remember that you are writing for highly-educated, widely-read, intellectually-curious people who have an intense desire for enriching interactions with their students. But if your expression is unclear and your argument obscure, you undermine the very possibility that this sort of interaction could occur.

You may find it useful, as you are writing your paper, to pretend that instead of turning it in to your instructor, you will be reading it to a wider audience of professors at your college. This will be a smart and engaged audience. Yet, it is unlikely that they will understand: (a) any technical jargon; (b) the intellectual context of the texts you are discussing; or (c) the value of the argument you want to make. You will have to define your terms, explain all quotations, justify all inferences, and state precisely the conclusion of your argument. Sometimes you can simulate this audience by showing or reading drafts of your papers to classmates, friends, or family members.

1.6 A Checklist for Spotting Problems Early

☑ Have you chosen a topic that:
   a) meets the requirements your instructor set for the assignment; and
   b) demonstrates your grasp of the primary source texts and issues covered in your class?

☑ Can you state in three sentences or less exactly what is the point of your paper?

☑ Can you explain specifically how your position fits in with the positions of philosophers with whom you generally agree?

☑ Can you explain where specifically your position differs from the positions of philosophers with whom you disagree?

☑ Can you explain why your view is preferable to the one you are criticizing on the issue(s) where you differ?

☑ Can you explain the view you are criticizing in a way that makes it sound like a reasonable view that an intelligent person could hold?

☑ Do you understand why the view you are criticizing was an important one to have been voiced, even if you think it is wrong?

☑ Can you state what impact you contribution should have, if it is correct, on the debate to which your paper contributes?

2

Philosophical Writing Advances a Thesis with an Argument

2.1 Consuming Arguments

1 What is an argument?

When philosophers talk about arguments, they are not talking about disagreements. If you are *having an argument* with someone, the two of you probably hold different views on some matter that is causing conflict. In the course of having an argument, it is possible that you would *make an argument* to your counterpart. When you make an argument, you assert that your view follows from good reasons.

Imagine that someone were writing down everything you and your counterpart said in the course of having an argument. Now, imagine that as you read over the transcript, you found two consecutive sentences where one sentence stated the reason supporting your view, and the other sentence stated your view. This two-membered set of sentences is an argument.

An argument consists of two parts: the premises and the conclusion.[1] The statements that provide reasons or support are the premises. The premises provide reasons for accepting a further statement as true, namely, the conclusion. Usually, there must be at least one premise.

---

[1] Technically, arguments can have one (and in the case of theorems, where the conclusion is a logically-valid sentence, zero) premises. Nonetheless, since most arguments have more than one, and for ease of exposition, I will discuss premis*es* in the plural.

There can only be one conclusion per argument.[2] Arguments come in two main varieties: *deductive* and *inductive*.

DEDUCTIVE ARGUMENTS

Philosophers tend to present what they study and what they produce as *deductive arguments*. In a deductive argument, the premises are supposed to provide conclusive support for the conclusion. Arguments that succeed in doing this are called deductively *valid* arguments. An argument is deductively valid if and only if, if the premises are true, then the conclusion must be true. Notice that the premises do not have to be true. But if they are true, it is impossible for the conclusion to be false. Consider the following example.

Premise 1:	All men are mortal.
Premise 2:	Socrates is a man.
Conclusion:	Therefore, Socrates is mortal.

It would be inconsistent to maintain the truth of the two premises, and yet to deny the truth of the conclusion. To deny the conclusion is to maintain that Socrates is not mortal, and affirming the second premise is saying that Socrates is a man. Thus, there would be *at least one man who is not* mortal, namely, Socrates. However, the first premise states that *all men are* mortal and that must (by the second premise) include Socrates. If all men are mortal, then there cannot be some man (Socrates) who is not mortal. So one cannot consistently affirm both premises and deny the conclusion. *That* is what we call a deductively valid argument.

INDUCTIVE ARGUMENTS

Alternatively, in an inductive argument, the premises provide *some* support – but not conclusive support – for the conclusion. As opposed to a deductive argument, where the conclusion follows necessarily from the premises, an inductive argument is one where the conclusion follows from the premises with some degree of *probability*. Inductive

---

[2] Complex arguments sometimes contain as premises the conclusions of other arguments. Since these conclusions are demonstrated "along the way" to the ultimate conclusion, they are often called "intermediate conclusions." But they are still conclusions of discrete arguments.

arguments can be more or less strong. An inductively strong argument with true premises is a *cogent* inductive argument.

THE PREMISES SUPPORT THE CONCLUSION

The important general point to absorb about the relationship between the premises and conclusion of an argument is that the premises provide support for the conclusion. The orthodox view of logic explains this supporting relationship in terms of *truth*: a good argument invariably leads us from true statements to other true statements. Deductively valid arguments are *truth preserving* in that a statement that is *validly* inferred[3] from true premises *must be* true. Inductive arguments are *truth promoting* in that a statement that is *cogently* inferred from true premises is *very likely* true.

HOW BAD CAN AN "ARGUMENT" BE AND STILL COUNT AS AN ARGUMENT?

How you can tell whether a set of sentences constitutes an argument? If the only thing we say about an inductive argument is that the premises provide *some* support for the conclusion, without saying *how much* support, there seems to be a risk of treating almost any set of sentences as an argument. Consider whether the following set of sentences is an argument:

(Supposed premise)   (1)   Smith is wearing a shirt.
(Supposed conclusion)   (2)   Smith is wearing blue.

Suppose that 80 percent of the shirts Smith owns and wears are blue, so it is quite likely that, if he is wearing a shirt, then he is wearing

---

[3]   There is some tension between two alternative ways of describing arguments. The first way describes arguments as sets of sentences where the premises bear a certain relationship to the conclusion; namely, whenever the premises are true, the conclusion also has to be true. The second way describes arguments as the sort of thing that people can make when they are reasoning correctly, where the conclusion is validly inferred from the premises when a person who is justified in asserting the premises is for that reason alone justified in asserting the conclusion. The first way has no need to talk about inferences, because validity is a property of certain sets of sentences rather than a property of reasoning from one sentence to another. Some philosophers call this a difference between a static and a dynamic conception of logic. See Shapiro (1997), especially Chapter 6.

blue. But, if you had never met Smith, and knew nothing of the contents of his wardrobe, and you offered (1) in support of (2) to someone else who was similarly ignorant of his habitual mode of dress, it would be an abuse of the term to think that you had made an *argument*. By asserting (1), you would not have offered a reason to accept that (2) is true.

One response to this problem is to say that the speaker must *intend* that the sentences be construed as an argument. But since the question whether one sentence provides support for another has nothing to do with *whether the speaker intends* one statement to provide support for another, this response is a nonstarter. Another option is to say that two sentences constitute an argument *if the audience thinks that* one sentence supports the other. But what the audience thinks is just as irrelevant as what the speaker intends to the question whether the premises actually provide support for the conclusion.

The problem is that the fact that Smith is wearing a shirt provides support for the conclusion that Smith is wearing blue *only if we know a few additional facts about Smith's dressing habits*. A sentence may be a constituent part of an explanation without constituting an explanation by itself; and, likewise, a sentence may be a constituent part of some support for a conclusion without constituting support for a conclusion by itself. In the case at hand, if someone offered (1) *Smith is wearing a shirt* and offered an additional premise (1.5) *80 percent of the shirts worn by Smith are blue*, then we would have an argument, since the premises (1) and (1.5) together provide support for believing (2) *Smith is wearing blue*.

Some would not agree that it is an abuse of the term to say that "(1), therefore (2)" is an argument, given the very simple fact that it is impossible that Smith is wearing blue if Smith is not wearing anything at all. So, to follow this tack, if someone knew that (1) *Smith is wearing a shirt*, then she would be slightly more justified in believing that (2) *Smith is wearing blue* than she would be if she were entirely ignorant of whether or not he had dressed. However, this objection proves too much. For, it is also impossible that Smith is wearing blue if he does not exist. So offering (3) *Smith exists* would, on this line of reasoning, seem to provide another bit of justification for believing (2) *Smith is wearing blue*.

The suggestion that *Smith exists; therefore Smith is wearing blue* is an argument strikes me as ridiculous. Knowing that Smith exists is a reason for thinking that Smith has some properties, but not for thinking that he has the specific property of wearing blue. Consider the following parallel example. If we want to verify whether the Loch Ness Monster is green, we may first want to inquire whether there is a Loch Ness Monster. However, we do so not because that will be evidence that it is green, but because it will convince us that we are not wasting our time looking for evidence as to its hue.

The reason it is so difficult to make any progress in deciding how much support a premise must offer a conclusion in order for "[premise], therefore [conclusion]" to qualify as an argument is that it does not make a lot of sense to talk about *what is a justification for what* in the abstract. Depending on the method of inquiry and the subject matter studied, certain facts will be relevant to the justification of certain beliefs and others will not. So I think the question "Do these sentences constitute an argument?" has to be asked with some awareness of what sort of statement the conclusion is and what counts as a justification for accepting it in the context of a particular mode of inquiry. I will come back to this question in the next section when I discuss "the assertibility question."

WHICH SORT OF ARGUMENT DO PHILOSOPHERS TEND TO MAKE?

Philosophers frequently make deductive arguments. Sketching out which premises could be offered to provide conclusive support for a conclusion is one of our best tools for explicating what it might mean for the conclusion to be true. However, making deductive arguments often plays a more prominent role in explaining and criticizing a position than it does in defending one. Thus, to the extent that you aim to propose and defend a view in your papers, rather than explain or criticize one, you will spend most of your effort making inductive rather than deductive arguments. For example, in my dissertation, my main argument was something like this:

(1) If Tarski's account of logical consequence is adequate, then it must explain valid reasoning.
(2) But it does not.
(3) Therefore, Tarski's account of logical consequence is inadequate.

That is a simple, deductively valid argument. However, that argument took three lines to state, and the dissertation was 230 pages. So why did I bother spilling all that ink?

The answer is that I had to make as persuasive a case as I could that my premises are true. In the course of making that case, I made many deductive arguments. But it would be inaccurate to say that I gave a *proof* that my conclusion is true. The most I could claim for the arguments I offered was that (assuming they worked) they proved conclusions that *provide support for* my main premises. I made all the good arguments I could think up (and built on some arguments that others had thought up) in order to provide reasons to think that premises (1) and (2) are both true. Furthermore, I tried to show the advantages of my position for logical theory and the disadvantages of several alternative positions that I think are wrongheaded. Thus, I think students of philosophy do well to think of themselves not as intellectual Euclids who start with indubitable propositions and deduce the necessary consequences in true geometrical fashion, but rather as participants in rational inquiry, ready to cobble together the best case they can for their views from whatever evidence and arguments they can muster.

2 How is a philosopher's argument to be recognized?

The first step in recognizing a philosopher's argument is identifying the *thesis* that is being developed in the passage you are reading. Philosophers tend to write articles and books because they think that certain statements are true. These statements are the results of the philosopher's research. They are the insights the author wants the reader to glean from the text. Philosophical texts usually have one global thesis – the statement that the text as a whole is supposed to prove – as well as many local theses – the conclusions of the many supporting arguments that the author makes for the global thesis. You may have to read a passage several times in order to discover its role in the argument. But once you have discovered the statement the author is mainly trying to prove, you will have discovered the author's global thesis.

The next step is to try to find the premises that, if true, would provide support for the thesis/conclusion. Some contemporary authors are kind enough just to tell us what their premises are, and explain why the conclusion follows from them. Alas, this is not generally the case, which makes more work for the reader. A good way to discover the argument the author is making is to ask:

☑ What reasons has the author given me to accept this conclusion?

It may be necessary to search for the argument using other questions as well. You might also ask:

☑ Why did the author accept the conclusion?

or

☑ What other commitments of the author entitled him or her to accept the conclusion?

Alec Fisher (2004: 22) has suggested asking what he calls "the assertibility question":

☑ "What argument or evidence would justify me in asserting the conclusion? (What would I have to know or believe to be justified in accepting it?)"

These questions are helpful to ask in order to think about what *an* argument for the author's conclusion would have to look like.

However, the argument *the author gave the reader* in his or her text or the argument *the author accepted him- or herself* may be different than *what you would have to know or believe* to be justified in accepting the conclusion. Sometimes your ideas about what it takes to be justified in believing a proposition are different from the author's. If you are trying to discover what the author's argument is, you have to be attentive to the fact that the author may not have made the best argument he or she could have for the conclusion. Noticing this difference is a great advantage, since it would make an excellent philosophy paper to explain the author's argument and then explain why a different argument for the same conclusion would have been better. Nonetheless, if you ask what would justify belief in the author's conclusion, and then re-read the author's text with this in mind, you are likely to identify those considerations that the author has offered in support of his or her conclusion.

3 The principle of charity

When you reconstruct an author's argument, try to attribute to him or her the strongest argument that can be supported by the text. You need to read and interpret accurately, but also charitably. Extremely smart people wrote the various texts you will be reading. So while you must respect the text, and support the views you attribute to the philosopher with quotations, if the argument you think you have found is *obviously* invalid or *embarrassingly* bad, then it is probably not the author's argument after all.

In philosophy, we reconstruct a philosopher's position in order to scrutinize it. Usually we criticize it too. But your scrutiny and criticism will be irrelevant if you are not considering arguments the author actually made. Do not waste time refuting a weak position that no one really defends, setting up a straw man[4] and then knocking it down. Moreover, if you want your interlocutor to care about your analysis, you have to show that you understand his or her position. In fact, you have to show that you understand the position at least as well as your interlocutor does. People are generally unreceptive to criticism, unless you can show that you understand the merits of their position:

> One can at the same time understand perfectly and disagree completely with what the other side is saying. But unless you can convince them that you do grasp how they see it, you may be unable to explain your viewpoint to them. Once you have made their case for them, then come back with the problems you find in their proposal. If you can put their case better than they can, and then refute it, you maximize the chance of initiating a constructive dialogue on the merits and minimize the chance of their believing you have misunderstood them (Fisher, Ury, and Patton 1991: 35).

---

[4] When a person mischaracterizes one side of an argument so as to discredit it more easily, he or she is said to commit the "straw man" fallacy, because the position that has been mischaracterized only seems to be a real position, just as a scarecrow only seems (to the birds) to be a real person.

If the goal of your paper is to critically engage your opponent's view with your own, you will be successful only if you have fairly and accurately reconstructed your opponent's view.

Another reason you should aim to reconstruct the best argument the text will support is that philosophers, such as you, often cull important insights from theories or conceptions they nevertheless think are flawed. Sometimes the conception a philosopher has developed enables you to consider an old problem in a new light – to think that the mind is just the brain or that existence is not a property or that pleasure is the essence of the good – even if one takes issue with the arguments the philosopher offered to support his or her insight. The activity of carefully reconstructing a philosopher's argument often permits us to see precisely where thinker went wrong – to diagnose the faulty inference, the shaky premise, or the inapt concept. The payoff is that you may then try to improve upon the argument by offering your own original explanation that sets the insight upon a sounder rational foundation. That is to say, careful reading, charitable interpretation, and accurate reconstruction of an argument are often the first steps towards making some philosophical progress of your own.[5]

In applying the principle of charity, you might to try to think of one or two things for which you can be grateful to the author in order to identify the merits of his or her view. Probably the author clarified something or moved the discussion in a new or interesting direction. Identifying what the author did manage to accomplish will help you to be sure that you have not missed his or her point entirely, even if you think that the project is a miserable failure. If a text seems facile or boring, and that is all you take away from reading it, you have certainly missed what your instructor wanted you to get from having read it.

Surprisingly, the more influential a philosopher has been, sometimes the more difficult it is to see what is so interesting about his or her arguments. When a perspective has been so completely absorbed into common sense, it can be difficult to recognize that it was probably a monumental accomplishment to express that perspective coherently and persuasively for the first time. It helps, therefore, to have some

---

[5] I was prompted to make this point after reading Alisdair MacIntyre (2006).

sense of the intellectual milieu in which the author worked in order to appreciate what were the problems he or she was trying to address, what were the available modes for addressing such problems, and what would have changed in his or her era had everyone accepted the arguments.

4 How is an argument to be criticized?

GOOD STRATEGIES

There are several ways to criticize an argument, but the most obvious are these: (a) show that the conclusion does not follow from the premises; or (b) show that one or more of the premises is false. First, if it is possible to grant an author's premises and deny his or her conclusion, then the argument is invalid. This means that *even if* the premises are true (not saying yet whether they are), they would not constitute sufficient evidence to prove the conclusion true. One species of this criticism is to show that the author proved something other than what he or she was aiming to prove. Remember that the conclusion might still be true. But if the argument is invalid, then *that argument* does not provide sufficient reasons for taking the conclusion to be true.

Alternatively, if one of the premises is false, then the author has not provided adequate support for the conclusion, even if the argument is valid. An argument points up what must be the case in a world that is correctly described by the premises. However, if the actual world is not correctly described by the premises – that is, the factual basis asserted in the premises is spurious – then regardless of any necessary connections between the premises and conclusion, the argument fails to point up something that must be the case. The strategy described in the previous paragraph is the primary way to criticize an inference contained in an argument. The strategy described in this paragraph is the primary way to criticize the factual foundation upon which the inference is based.

There is another way to criticize an argument, which does not involve showing that the argument is invalid but rather that its validity is uninteresting because the argument is circular. If I say "God exists; therefore, God exists," I will have provided a valid argument, because it is impossible that the premise is true but the conclusion false. But this is a hollow victory indeed. Anyone who does not already accept the conclusion would not accept the premise I offered to support it. I have assumed what I was supposed to prove – and assumptions, as Bertrand Russell once observed, have all "the advantages of theft over honest toil" ([1919] 1993: 71).

You will never encounter, in a serious philosophical work, a circular argument that is as baldly stated as the one above. However, you are well-advised to be on the lookout for philosophical arguments that "beg the question," in that the truth of (one of more of) the premises depends *implicitly* or *indirectly* on the truth of the conclusion. Or, what is perhaps more common still, the truth of (one or more of) the premises that figure in one philosopher's argument may *assume the falsity* of his or her opponent's view. For example, consider the following argument, with obvious bearing on the morality of abortion:

Premise 1:	The biological identity of a human individual is fixed at fertilization.
Premise 2:	Any human individual is a human person.
First Conclusion:	A human person exists at fertilization.
Premise 3:	All human persons deserve respect for their lives and equality before the law.
Second Conclusion:	From fertilization, all human persons deserve respect for their lives and equality before the law.

The first premise makes an empirical claim about the point in the development of a zygote at which it is a single, identifiable, individuated life with determinate genetic characteristics. Let us assume that this claim is true, in order to focus our attention solely on the second premise. The second premise is not an empirical claim, but a metaphysical claim about what it means to be a human person. It is a claim that has its merits in understanding human personhood, and it might be true. However, it is very likely to be rejected by anyone who is not initially inclined to accept the conclusion. Some of those who believe that respect and legal recognition do not attach (or do not attach equally) to human beings at the early stages of development hold this view because it follows from a different understanding of human personhood. For example, some philosophers hold that a human being is a human person in virtue of his or her capacity for conscious experience and self-awareness of existing over time (Singer 2000: 217–18, 320) (endorsing James Rachels' distinction between a biographical and biological life); (Singer 1993: 87ff). Thus, they would reject Premise 2, because these capacities are not always enjoyed by each and every member of the species. They are, rather, capacities that emerge, develop and sometimes, tragically, fade away.

It is important to note that it is not a logical or empirical flaw of the argument that Premise 2 would likely be rejected by anyone not predisposed to accept the Second Conclusion. That is to say, the likely rejection of Premise 2 does not imply that it is false (and thus that the argument is unsound) or that the First Conclusion does not follow logically (and thus that the argument is invalid). Yet, insofar as this argument is supposed to make a rational claim upon us, irrespective of any prior views we may have had about the ultimate conclusion, it presents a dialectical shortcoming. This argument is likely to be offered in a context where those who are meant to be persuaded by the argument are likely to have reasonable reservations about one of the crucial steps. Thus, a person who offered this argument would, predictably, be ineffective in persuading the most obvious interlocutor, namely, one whose ultimate position differs on the matter of respect for life and equality before the law. It is a solid strategy of philosophical criticism to show of an argument that its rational purchase is limited to those who already accept a crucial, yet contested commitment that is perhaps too closely related to its ultimate conclusion to make any headway against someone with a different view.

BAD STRATEGIES

There is a fallacy (that is, a form of bad argument) called *argumentum ad hominem* in which a critic attacks the person instead of the person's position or argument. Stating of a philosopher that he or she holds strange views, or writes badly or is too abstract is not an adequate philosophical criticism. Being unrealistic or abstract or badly-put is different from being false or invalid.

Unless you are writing a book review (something that usually only graduate students and professional philosophers bother to do), it is bad form to praise or insult the author's achievement in writing the text. Perhaps the book or article has an annoying number of seemingly superfluous footnotes. Perhaps it is unfathomably dense or detailed. That makes for tedious reading, but it is ultimately irrelevant to both the soundness of argumentation offered in the text and to your critical appraisal of those arguments. Alternatively, perhaps the book or article changed your life somehow. In that case, write the author personally and let him or her know or recommend the book to everyone you care about. Nonetheless, except in those rare cases when that kind of personal assessment is an integral part of the thesis you plan to develop and defend in your paper, it does not belong in academic writing.

2.2 Producing Arguments

✒ 5 A clearly stated, tightly focused thesis is essential

Your thesis is the statement you want your reader to accept after having read your paper. It is the conclusion of your argument. Stating your thesis clearly and explicitly at the beginning of a paper is important for two reasons. First, the reader will know how to judge the success of a paper only if he or she knows what the paper sets out to accomplish. The thesis reveals to the reader the goal of the paper. In fact, some authors go so far as to tell the reader exactly how to judge the success of the paper: "This paper should be judged successful if I have succeeded in showing that Kant held such-and-such view for these-and-such reasons." Second, stating the thesis explicitly helps keep the author on task, since there is no confusion about the author's own purpose.

The thesis should be tightly focused. Almost every paper has to be written within certain word- or page-limits, and the author ought not to tackle a topic that cannot be suitably addressed in the allotted space. It is foolish to begin a five-page paper with the claim: "I will show that Kant's moral philosophy is wrong." This is brash and obviously unattainable. Why not write: "I will show that the argument Kant gives in *Groundwork* for his claim that the only thing that is properly called *good* is a good will is invalid." You might be able to do this in five pages, and it would be fascinating if you did.

6 The introduction states why you wrote the paper and why your audience should read it

The paper should have an introduction. The introduction should tell the reader the thesis you plan to defend and the strategy you will carry out in order to defend it. Think of it this way: by the end of your introduction the reader should know why you bothered to write the paper, and why he or she should bother to read it. If your paper does not have an introduction that accomplishes this, then the reader will be lost from the start. Now, you may have to introduce your topic or otherwise explain why you are writing the paper before you come clean with your goal and strategy. Yet, that sort of introductory commentary should only take a few paragraphs. So a statement of your thesis and an outline of your game plan should still come almost immediately at the start of your paper.

Whatever you do, never begin a paper with quasi-poetical platitudes concerning such bizarre topics as, for example, the psychological burdens of being a true philosopher or our glorious (or depraved) ancestors. Some writers seem to think that the reader might be brought under some kind of rhetorical spell by an opening paragraph that showcases the author's:

- ☑ vocabulary;
- ☑ breadth of reading;
- ☑ familiarity with a few highbrow phrases (usually in Latin);
- ☑ ability to wax eloquently on highly abstract topics;
- ☑ detailed knowledge of current or historical events;
- ☑ awareness of obscure conspiracy theories; or
- ☑ ability to be terribly idealistic or cynical.

On the contrary, any critical reader will see a giant red flag if the opening of a paper features any of these elements. Instead, introduce your reasons for choosing to write on your topic, and clearly state what you intend to accomplish in the paper and how.

Your papers should never simply recapitulate the text you are discussing. Your reader will have already read whatever you are discussing, so what reason would he or she have to read a mere recapitulation? (Yes, I know it is your instructor's job to read it, but that misses the point.) Imagine that before your instructor will agree to read your paper, you have to convince her that it is worth her valuable time. What would you say? Keep in mind, as you introduce your paper to the reader, what you take to be especially important or helpful about your paper. Give the reader some reason to think that her understanding of the author, text, or philosophical issues will be improved by reading your paper. And, most importantly, have confidence that you do indeed have something important to contribute to your reader's understanding of important authors, texts, and issues.

7 The body of your paper follows a strategy to demonstrate your thesis

Your argument provides the overall structure for your paper. Consequently, you should tell the reader what role each part of your paper plays in your argument. Transitions ought to be explicit. Your reader ought to know at every point in your paper what you have just accomplished, what you are up to now, and where you are going next. For example, when you have completed an argument, you might remind the reader of the basic structure of that argument, perhaps by briefly stating your conclusion, the premises from which it follows, and the *reasons why* it follows. The last bit (about the reasons why the conclusion follows from the premises) is the most important bit, from a philosopher's perspective; for anyone can *claim* that, for example, it is implicit in the concept of knowledge that a proposition cannot be known unless it is true; but only philosophical writing contains *explanation, demonstration* of why that is so (if it is).

You might begin a new section of your paper in a similar way, by briefly restating what the previous section contributed to your overall strategy. Regardless, it is essential that you explain to the reader why the next section is *invited*, indeed *positively required* by the previous section *if* you are to fulfill your ultimate purpose. It is perfectly acceptable to be so direct as to write in the following manner: "I have just argued that [conclusion], because [basic statement of the previous argument]. This result raises the further question whether [next step in your strategy], because [basic statement of why, given the results of the previous section, you have to establish something further in order to reach your ultimate conclusion]. Thus, this section addresses [the intermediate step you still need in order to establish your ultimate conclusion]." Obviously, the way I have laid this out is formulaic and dull. I would hope that someone writing with a concrete topic would make the transition somewhat more artfully. But the basic point remains, that you stand a much better chance of rationally convincing your reader if you are forthright with the structure and progress of your argument.

Remember that you have a plan. Every part of your paper is part of the strategy you are carrying out to establish your thesis. Sentences and paragraphs should never come streaming one after the other without a clear relationship between them. Neither the paper as a whole nor any of its constituent paragraphs should read like a bullet-point list. There ought to be a clear logical progression from one paragraph to the next and one section to the next.

New topics get new paragraphs. Not only is this point essential to guiding your reader through your argument, but it is also essential to making a sound argument. If you permit yourself to broach several topics in a single paragraph, it is unlikely that you will adequately support any one of those topics with sufficient explanation or evidence to solidify it as a building block for what follows. Lastly, you should make it plain to the reader which aspect of your argument is addressed by any topic you raise, what contribution it makes to your overall strategy.

If a paragraph establishes something that you do not need for your argument, then you have to throw it out, no matter how clever it is. Authors sometimes turn their work inside out to keep even a single sentence that they think is especially profound, no matter how irrelevant to or inconsistent with the overall purpose of the paper. Do not ruin your paper for one pithy remark. I have been told that creative writers sometimes start with one good line and (say) write an entire screenplay just to frame it. But often the privileged line originated in an entirely different context from which it had to be excised because it simply did not fit. So write down the brilliant thought that you cannot bear to discard and file it away as the impetus for your next masterwork. In the meantime, stay focused on the thesis of your present paper.

8 Consider objections to your view

Your paper will be much stronger if you can anticipate some potential objections to your thesis or your argument and show how these objections should be addressed. Coming to terms with the merits of an opposing view and showing why the balance of reasons still supports your view is an indispensable step in becoming entitled to your commitment, as Mill explained:

> He who knows only his own side of the case, knows little of that. His reasons may be good, and no one may have been able to refute them. But if he is equally unable to refute the reasons on the opposite side; if he does not so much as know what they are, he has no ground for preferring either opinion. The rational position for him would be suspension of judgment, and unless he contents himself with that, he is either led by authority, or adopts, like the generality of the world, the side to which he feels most inclination. (Mill [1859] 1989: 38)

Generally, your rational duty is to argue from the premises you have the best reasons to accept. This duty is not fulfilled by arguing merely from those premises that seem compelling to you. You also have to address the premises that seem compelling to your opponent. Only then will you have some assurance that you have not mistaken the conclusion that is the easiest for you to accept with the conclusion that is best-supported by the balance of reasons.

An objection to your thesis includes any reason, fact, or argument that casts doubt on the truth of your thesis. An objection to your argument includes any consideration that casts doubt on the truth of one or more of your premises or the validity of the argument. A few common forms of objection include:

- ☑ your argument supports a different conclusion from what is asserted;
- ☑ your argument follows from premises that we have better reasons to reject than to accept;
- ☑ your argument, in order to be valid, requires additional, unacknowledged premises that you have not demonstrated or that are far-fetched or false;

☑ your interpretation of a philosopher's views neglects important textual evidence or, while making sense of certain passages, cannot explain or accommodate others;

☑ your view, while cogent when considered by itself, would have unanticipated and unacceptable consequences in other areas; thus, the critic feels compelled to reconsider, for example, the way you posed the question you set out to address, whether your premises take into account all of the available data, whether there is a subtle misuse of or disagreement over important terminology, etc.

The intellectual virtue that you will have to practice is suspending, for a moment, your particular inclinations and commitments and asking whether any of these types of objections (or others) have some force against your argument. What reason could a well-informed, intelligent person have to reject your argument, in spite of the reasons you have offered to accept it? Remember that it will only be interesting to consider objections to your thesis or argument if you consider solid, interesting objections. However, sometimes facile objections gain sufficient currency in a discussion that it is appropriate (and sometimes even important) to subject them to searching criticism, in an effort to expose them as mere distractions. Nevertheless, it will usually be most profitable and interesting to consider the most cogent, well-developed objections of the keenest participants in the debate.

This is a good place to mention the fact that well-reasoned philosophical thinking contributes to, and usually requires, an intellectual community. As you consider the views of others, develop your own, and consider objections, try to find a balance between respect for the accomplishment of others, confidence in the merits of your project, and humility about your own results. First, do not write as though you have finally triumphed over a problem that has for ages befuddled lesser minds. Second, think of your paper as your contribution to a process of conjectures, refutations, revisions, and further challenges. Jeremy Waldron[6] has described the fruits of vigorous philosophical debate among participants who are conscious of their own fallibility in this spirit:

[6] Waldron is University Professor at New York University School of Law, and works and teaches primarily in the philosophy of law and politically philosophy. A list of his publications can be found at: <http://its.law.nyu.edu/faculty/profiles/index. cfm?fuseaction=cv.main&personID=26993>.

The interplay of arguments is expected to produce better theories that will form the basis for an even more vigorous debate, and so on. In these debates, each of us has a responsibility to take the perspective of the philosophical community as well as the perspective of the particular view she is defending. From the latter perspective, one is a passionate partisan of a particular theory. From the former perspective, however, one knows that it is wrong to expect any particular theory, no matter how attractive or well argued, to survive the process of debate unscathed. One recognizes that the debate has a point: to use collective interaction as a way of reaching towards complicated truth. Simple truths, self-evident truths may form in single minds, but complicated truths . . . emerge, in Mill's words, only 'by the rough process of a struggle between combatants fighting under hostile banners.' (Waldron 1993: 31; quoting Mill 1989: 49)

As you consider objections to your own views, try to do so from both perspectives mentioned by Waldron: first, the philosophical community, as you propose and consider the objection, and; second, your own, when you respond to it.

9 The conclusion of your paper explains the conclusion of your argument

When concluding your paper, be careful to draw only the conclusion your argument warrants. You are writing a paper in order to demonstrate something specific, so do not conclude by saying, "So we can see that Kant's ethics is interesting and has influenced lots of other philosophers." I assume that no one would bother to write a paper trying to establish *that*, since if it is false there is not much point in writing about Kant at all. The conclusion of your paper should restate the thesis you have defended, briefly explain how you have argued for it, and indicate what you take to be the significance of your results in the context of the broader discussion of your topic. Furthermore, do not write a paper showing that one of Kant's arguments is invalid, and then conclude that you have refuted Kant's moral philosophy. That will be false, and it will appear that you do not understand the import of your own argument.

The conclusion should not come abruptly. It should be obvious to the reader when you are finished, because you have done everything you said you would do when you laid out the game plan in your introduction. Even if your paper raises more questions than it answers, you will want to show why the truth of your thesis raises these questions in particular, and why they are important and interesting. It is perfectly acceptable (and quite helpful) to identity as worthy of further research both the presuppositions of your own argument and implications of your argument that you have not had the opportunity to explore in your present paper.

10 On words that indicate conclusions and premises

Words such as "therefore," "thus," "hence," and "consequently" tell the reader that the statement that follows is the conclusion *of an argument*. Likewise, words such as "because" and "for" indicate that the statement that follows is the premise *of an argument*. If you use words that indicate the presence of either premises or a conclusion, make sure that they are attached to statements that function as premises or a conclusion (respectively) in your argument.

Do not confuse a sequential progression (what comes after what in some order of presentation) with logical progression (what can be inferred from what). Philosophers take arguments very seriously. We get excited when we read "therefore . . ." If it turns out that you have not really argued for the statement following "therefore," we will resent having been teased.

11 Provide justification for every important claim

If anything important in your paper rides on a particular claim being true, then you had better give the reader some reason to think that it is true. If nothing important in your paper rides on a particular claim being true, then why on earth is it in your paper? You should avoid what are sometimes called "throw-away comments" – statements that you are not prepared to justify and that do not affect the success of your main argument. Depending on your argument, it *might* be appropriate to mention matters of common sense or extremely basic facts ("the earth is round," for example), if only to provide an example or some context for claims that are integral to your argument. It will most likely be unnecessary to provide any support for such pedestrian claims. But if your argument is driving your exposition, chances are that you will need every allotted word to explain your inferences and justify your load-bearing premises.

By the way, saying that "most people think such-and-such" is totally irrelevant in almost all arguments. And it is certainly not a reason for your reader to think such-and-such. It is especially annoying to find this sort of statement in a philosophy paper, since precisely what is at issue in philosophical argument is what people are *justified* in thinking, that is, what they have *good reason* to think. Philosophers sometimes "plumb intuitions" to get a sense of what might approximate the right answer to a question. But nothing philosophically significant follows from the mere fact that somebody happens to have certain thoughts or intuitions.

Sometimes students tell quasi-mythological stories such as, "The founding fathers of the United States thought that . . ." or "Before there were governments . . ." Do not treat writing a philosophy paper as story time. If your argument relies on certain historical claims, then get them right. You had better have a historical source handy to support your claim. And you have to make it clear how such a claim advances your argument for a philosophically-interesting conclusion.

12 What makes an argument philosophically interesting?

As I explain in more detail in Chapter 8, philosophically-interesting arguments explicate the content of our concepts and evaluate the justifications we have for applying them as we do. It is not enough simply to make a valid argument in your paper. You have to explain something about how we should understand things or what we are right to think or do.

Consider this valid argument: "If what the Bible says is true, then abortion is wrong; what the Bible says is true; therefore, abortion is wrong." This argument by itself is valid and yet of very little philosophical interest, primarily for two reasons. First, the premises are terribly controversial. Philosophers will be interested in this argument only if they have been given some *reason* to accept the premises. Demonstrating that the first premise (the conditional statement) is true would require biblical exegesis to demonstrate that the Bible addresses abortion at all, states that it is wrong, etc. But, even if you could marshal the requisite evidence to support the first premise, and do so within the page or word limit of your paper (as opposed to a book), demonstrating that the second premise is true would require a complicated account of what it means for scripture, at least parts of which are explicitly poetic or otherwise literary, to be true. All of this is, however, only what it would take to *explain* what it means for the Bible *to be* true. You still have to *argue* that *it is* true. Appreciating the truth of scripture might very well require something like personal revelation; and, no matter how good your paper is, it won't accomplish that!

By no means am I suggesting that philosophy papers cannot build upon scriptural exegesis or investigate the application of the concept of truth to scripture. The point is that, if you expect your reader to take an interest in your reasoning and the conclusions you draw, you must build upon claims your reader understands and has reason to believe. If your reader might not already understand or believe them, you have a lot of work to do. A writer cannot sweep these issues under the rug – issues such as what it means for scripture to be *true* and how we might *know* of some piece of scripture *that it is* true – and expect the result to be a philosophically interesting paper.

The second reason that this argument is of very little philosophical interest is that, even assuming for the sake of argument that the conclusion is true, we do not learn anything about *why* abortion is wrong, what it means for abortion *to be wrong*, other than *that the Bible says so*. Like many arguments from authority, including the ones you have had with your parents when they say "because I said so," this argument does not *explain* anything. Philosophers want arguments that help us to understand *why* things are the way the conclusion says they are. Again, I am not saying that a philosophically-interesting paper could not be written about biblical ethics and abortion. The point is that such a paper would not aim at making the lame and question-begging argument mentioned above. A philosophically-interesting paper would explicate the concept of truth as applied to scripture, the concept of knowledge as applied to moral truths, the philosophical anthropology underlying biblical ethics or the distinction between justified and unjustified killing that issues from such an ethics; and it would build upon such explication of concepts or arguments or theories to form valid conclusions about problems of deep moral, human relevance, such as abortion. However, there is no sign of this sort of investigation in the trite little *modus ponens* we considered above.

Philosophers generally share a feeling of critical remove (at least initially) from concepts and justifications that are "traditionally" accepted. Philosophers feel compelled to think things through afresh, on their own. The conclusions of religious, political, or other authorities do not replace or foreclose independent, rational investigation. Being *unconstrained* by authority in doing philosophy is perfectly compatible with *respecting* and even *accepting* authorities after duly examining their legitimacy.

With respect to the relationship between authority and the pursuit of truth, philosophers tend to agree with John Stuart Mill, when he wrote: "Truth gains more even by the errors of one who, with due study and preparation, thinks for himself, than by the true opinions of those who only hold them because they do not suffer themselves to think" (1989: 36). After all, deference to authority is a *decision*; it is something for which we are *responsible*; and thus, it is a decision that we have to *justify* vis-à-vis our rational and moral obligations.

It is, however, a misunderstanding to think that autonomy and rationality exist only in competition and conflict with authority and revealed truth. Tradition and faith often make available concepts, conceptions, arguments, or even something as basic as a vocabulary, which facilitate our grasp of rational insights. But whatever there is to gain from the pursuit of truth and the love of wisdom only becomes yours by pursuing truth and loving wisdom. Other people cannot undergo your enlightenment for you – and you should not let them if they try.

People are sometimes struck by the desire to think things through on their own when the traditions they used to accept begin to seem strange or undesirable. Maybe you discover a fact that shows your tradition to have been crueler than it cares to advertise. Maybe a leader you respected is found out to have been a fraud. Maybe the commitments that anchored your way of life start to drift and begin to appear less necessary and increasingly optional. Experiences such as these tend to give a person anxiety about the answers they had to questions they inherited. And they often feel the need to reevaluate both the questions and the answers.

Whether or not you feel this need, philosophers tend to feel it acutely. Many people do experience something like "existential crisis" at some point in their lives, where this need is intensely felt. And although you may be satisfied with the answers given by family, religion, or a political ideology, a philosophy instructor will want to see you come to your conclusions through an independent and rational process, based on publicly-available evidence and supported by careful reasoning.

3

The Rudiments of Academic Writing

3.1 Elements of Style

13 Use the first-person, active voice

Writing in the first-person involves using the word "I" to refer to the subject active, as opposed to using words like "you" (the second-person) or "it" (the third-person). Writing in the active voice means writing about subjects who do things, as opposed to writing in the passive voice, that is, writing about events that happen to subjects. It will be much easier to think about your paper if you allow yourself to write in the first-person, active voice, especially in the first few paragraphs when you are setting up your thesis and strategy. That is to say, you should state somewhere in your introduction: "I will argue in this paper that [insert thesis]."

Writing in the passive voice ("it will be shown" or its ilk) can cause the author to lose sight of where the paper *needs* to go, or where the author *wants* the paper to go, because passive-voice constructions make is seem as though the paper has a life of its own. Sometimes writing feels this way. But when it does, it is time to stop and refocus. After all, papers do not write themselves. Similarly, writing "the purpose of this paper is . . ." can cause the author to believe that the sentences of the paper are automatically building toward a conclusion, when in fact the author is the one doing the building in accordance with his or her plan.

Sometimes using the passive voice can be a useful way to add variety to your prose or to make your paper sound a little less aggressive.

Sometimes you do not want to attribute the action in a sentence to anyone in particular, and in this case the passive voice might be appropriate. But it is more difficult to say something specific and clear in passive-voice constructions than active-voice constructions. Furthermore, the reader may think that you are using the passive voice and third-person pronouns to distance yourself as the author from the view you are explaining. Your writing will be clearer if you take ownership explicitly of what happens in your paper by using the first person, active voice.

14 Avoid using a conversational tone

You should read your paper aloud to yourself at least once before turning it in. This usually enables you to catch any awkward sentences, strange expressions, or incomplete or underdeveloped sentences before your instructor does. The moral here is that sometimes when we read over a paper we read right over mistakes. We are less likely to pass over a mistake when we hear it, probably because reading aloud is a more deliberate activity, so we are paying better attention.

However, this advice should not be misconstrued as recommending that we write the way we talk. Remember your task and your audience. Academic writing usually requires a serious tone – though by "serious" I do not mean *heavy*. Philosophical texts sometimes contain jokes, but usually they are jokes that reveal something important about the topic at hand. What is ruled out by "a serious tone" includes abusing a philosopher for his or her views or a text for being difficult or using examples that are crazy or offensive when mentioning something crazy or offensive is not required by the argument.

15 The paper should have a title

The title of your paper should serve as an invitation to your reader to think in a particular way about the topic of your paper. Does your paper struggle with a difficult question? If so, then maybe your title should ask that question. Are you going to advance and defend a thesis? If so, then maybe your title should state that thesis or at least the major concepts that your thesis involves. Are you offering an interpretation of a philosopher's views on some subject? If so, then the philosopher's name or the title of his or her work should probably appear somewhere in the title, along with the major concepts or issues to be discussed.

Under no circumstances should you disgrace your essay with a stupid, corny title. Lame titles tell the reader that you lack respect for the assignment, your reader, and (most regrettably) your own intellectual work.

16 Pages should be numbered

Page numbers will facilitate reference to specific passages of your paper when your reader is writing comments and making suggestions. Probably no one really cares where on the page the page numbers appear, so long as they are easy to spot and unobtrusive.

17 The correct use of punctuation

- ☑ A *comma* (,) is used before a conjunction (such as "and" or "but") joining two independent clauses, to set off parenthetical remarks, and whenever else you want to indicate that one part of the sentence is independent of another part.
- ☑ A *semi-colon* (;) is used to join two independent clauses, especially if the second clause begins with a transition such as "however," "nevertheless," etc. It looks like a period placed over a comma, and the semi-colon combines their functions in that what comes before and after could stand on their own as sentences (hence the period function), yet are so closely related in your exposition that they belong together (hence the comma function).
- ☑ A *colon* (:) is used to introduce a list, a definition, or an explanation of a term.
- ☑ An *em dash* (– or —) is used like parentheses when it is used in formal writing. That is, it sets off commentary, asides or clarifications from the rest of the sentence. Em dashes may also be used at the end of a sentence to add further amplification, qualification, observation, support, or, sometimes, rhetorical flourish. Consider the following passage from Kant: "For enlightenment of this kind [that is, "emergence from self-incurred immaturity"], all that is needed is *freedom*. And the freedom in question is the most innocuous form of all—freedom to make *public use* of one's reason in all matters" ([1784] 1991: 55).

Used in this way, the em dash functions just the same as a colon.[1]

18 The correct use of Latin abbreviations

There are a few Latin abbreviations that commonly appear in the body of a paper:

- ☑ "*e.g.*" abbreviates "*exempli gratia*," which means "for example."
- ☑ "*ibid.*" abbreviates "*ibidem*," which means "in the same place" (used when referring to the text that was cited in the immediately-preceding reference).
- ☑ "*i.e.*" abbreviates "*id est*," which means "that is" (used when explaining a term or statement immediately preceding).

Place a comma after each use of one of these abbreviations. Many writers only use these three. But there are several others that commonly appear in footnotes or parenthetical citations:

- ☑ "cf." abbreviates "confer," which means "consult" or "compare," but not "see also" (for which, write "see also").
- ☑ "*et al.*" abbreviates "*et alii*," which means "and others" (usually used when a book has multiple editors or a view has multiple expositors or adherents).
- ☑ "*loc. cit.*" abbreviates "*loco citato*," which means "in the place cited" (used when referring to the same specific *place* in a text previously cited).
- ☑ "*NB*" abbreviates "*nota bene*," which means "note well" (used when you especially want the reader to notice something).
- ☑ "*op. cit.*" abbreviates "*opere citato*," which means "in the work cited" (used, for example, when referring to a part of a text whose bibliographical information has just been given in the same footnote or the one immediately preceding and generally follows mention of the author's name).

---

[1]   The best reference I reviewed to prepare this section was *The Chicago Manual of Style* (University of Chicago Press Staff 2003: see ch. 6). Incidentally, the "em" in "em dash" refers to the width of a capital M in 12-point font.

☑ "*viz.*" abbreviates "*videlicet,*" "namely" (used when instructing the reader how something should be interpreted).[2]

⟋ 19 The correct use of Latin expressions

There are many Latin expressions that serve as technical terms in philosophy. I shall not try to explain them, for (as I explain in ⟋ 42) explanations of technical terminology must be faithful to the philosophical context in which they occur. The expressions I explain in this section are commonly used in philosophical writing; yet, they are merely fancy terms, not philosophical terms. (Foreign language words should be italicized, and usually abbreviations of foreign language words are too.)

a fortiori	*ex hypothesi*	*passim*
ad hoc	*ex post facto*	*per se*
bona fide	*ipso facto*	*prima facie*
ceteris paribus	*magnum opus*	*qua*
de facto	*modus operandi*	*sine qua non*
de jure	*mutatis mutandis*	*sui generis*
ex ante	*pace*	

The expression "*a fortiori*" means "even more conclusively." It is used to introduce a statement when you have just given a reason that supports one conclusion (stated in the preceding sentence or clause), and you think that this same reason is especially strong support for what you are about to say next (stated in the next sentence or clause). Example: "The fact that zygotes do not exhibit consciousness does not show that they are not human persons, and, *a fortiori*, does not show that they have a different moral status than any of us."

The expression "*ad hoc*" is used to describe a proposition that does not follow naturally from a particular theory, but is or appears to be fabricated for the specific purpose of addressing a pesky problem that would otherwise confound the theory. It is usually used in a pejorative sense to indicate that although the response might be fine on its own, it does not appear to be a consequence of the theory in question. Example: "Quantum phenomena cannot be explained within contemporary thermodynamics, but are accommodated by supplementing the theory with additional *ad hoc* hypotheses."

The expression "*bona fide*" is used to indicate that a proposition was asserted "in good faith." In addition, "*bona fide*" is frequently used to mean "genuine" in the sense of "actual" or "in good standing." Example: "It is open to question whether the Churchlands are *bona fide* eliminative materialists."

The expression "*ceteris paribus*" means "everything else being equal." It is used to indicate that an application of an explanatory generalization is valid only on the assumption that the *explanandum* (that is, the thing that is being explained) is a typical case. By definition, exceptions are not covered by the rule. Example: "Evidence that a prisoner attempted to escape custody is evidence, *ceteris paribus*, of a guilty conscience."

The expression "*de facto*" means "of fact" and is used to indicate that a state-of-affairs obtains as a matter of fact rather than a matter of right or law (that is, "*de jure*"). Example: "The fact that several of the states that have the death penalty have not executed a death-eligible prisoner in almost 30 years shows that most states have abolished the death penalty *de facto*, even if it remains a permissible penal sanction *de jure*."

The expression "*ex ante*" means "beforehand" and is used to refer to the situation before some critical event. Example: "Given that it is impossible to predict *ex ante* exactly how one's actions will affect the well-being of others, it is difficult to see how the utilitarian maxim 'Act so as to maximize general utility' could be of much use to a moral agent contemplating her next act."

The expression "*ex hypothesi*" means "by hypothesis" and is used to indicate that some proposition is assumed to be true by the position being discussed. Example: "However, the materialist has to explain the phenomenon of consciousness in terms of brain-states, for *ex hypothesi* the only things that exist are material things."

The expression "*ex post facto*" means "after the fact" and is used to indicate the opposite situation of *ex ante*. Example: "The utilitarian is, consequently, only in a position to evaluate the morality of actions *ex post facto*, which may be useful in writing history, but is less so in life."

The expression "*ipso facto*" means "by that fact" and is used to indicate that the existence of one fact is a sufficient condition for the existence of another. Example: "The agent acted as a virtuous person would act and *ipso facto* did what is morally right."

The expression "*magnum opus*" means "great work" and is used to refer to an author's crowning achievement. Example: "*Making It Explicit*, Robert Brandom's *magnum opus*, explains the Kantian roots of his theory of inferentialism."

The expression "*modus operandi*" means "mode of operation" and refers to one's typical practice. Example: "Passivity can be a provoking *modus operandi*; Consider the Empire and Gandhi" (Nash 1948).

The expression "*mutatis mutandis*" means "things being changed that need to be changed." It is used to indicate that an explanation you just offered for one phenomenon would also explain another phenomenon, although certain changes would need to be made in the expression of the explanation to make it fit the new target. Example: "The criticism of model-theoretic semantics offered by Etchemendy applies, *mutatis mutandis*, to any theory of logic on which arguments are valid in virtue of their logical form."

The expression "*pace*" is used to indicate that someone (maybe you) disagree with someone else. Example: "I will argue that an action can produce the greatest good for the greatest number of people and still be morally wrong, *pace* Mill."

"*Passim*" means "throughout" and usually appears in citations to indicate that a particular idea or word occurs in many places in the cited text, thus making pinpoint citation tedious.

The expression "*per se*" means "as such" in the sense of "essentially" or sometimes in the sense of "itself." It is used to indicate that something has a property simply in virtue of *being what it is* and not because of any other facts. Example 1: "A self-contradictory statement is *per se* false." Example 2: "Causal connections are never grasped by the senses *per se*."

The expression "*prima facie*" means "on its face" and is used to indicate that something initially appears to have a property, although further consideration or additional evidence might show it to be otherwise. Example: "Killing an innocent person is *prima facie* immoral, though some argue that if it would somehow prevent a nuclear holocaust, it might be morally permissible notwithstanding."

The expression "*qua*" means "considered as" and is used to indicate that something has a property in its specific capacity as such-and-such a sort of thing. Example: "One is *qua* philosopher concerned with explicating concepts and justifying commitments."

The expression "*sine qua non*" means "something indispensable," literally "without which not." Example: "It is a *sine qua non* of any adequate theory of meaning that it explains what a person knows if he or she understands a sentence."

The expression "*sui generis*" means "of its own kind" in the sense of unique and irreducible. Example: "Consciousness is a *sui generis* property that cannot be eliminated from an explanation of the mind by exclusively studying neurophysiology."

20 The consistent use of pronouns

If you say, "A person . . . ," then use "he or she" to refer to the subject, not "they." "They" is a plural pronoun. If you use "One might hold . . . ," then say "one would be wrong" not "they would be wrong." I have come across some sentences in papers that used "one" then "he/she" and then "they," all referring to the same subject. That is silly and confusing. Be consistent. The motivation for using "they" when "he or she" is appropriate is to remain gender neutral while using fewer words. Sexist language should, of course, never be used. But there is simply no need to write in a confusing way to avoid it.

21 Grammatical errors

As a rule, philosophers tend not to be overly hung-up on grammatical niceties. Ending sentences with prepositions ("Kant's ethics is the topic that I will focus *on*") and splitting infinitives ("It is impossible *to* coherently *argue* for relativism") tend to be mistakes and should probably be avoided. But it is a pretty rare occasion when these mistakes affect the plain sense of a sentence. Sometimes an author turns a sentence inside out in order not to end with a preposition, thereby obscuring the meaning of the sentence. The most famous send-up of this habit was when Winston Churchill said that such tortured composition was something "up with which I will not put." Obviously, this is silly. Grammar is the system of rules that facilitate meaningful expression. If you sacrifice clear meaning in order to follow a grammatical rule, then you have really missed the point of grammar.

Nevertheless, given that philosophers prize clarity and precision of expression so highly, it is important that you avoid grammatical errors that do detract from the meaningfulness of your exposition. Sometimes a paper submitted by an otherwise mindful student contains a sentence without a verb. Never let a mistake remain in your written work that would prompt the reader to question your literacy. Other papers contain such sentences as, "Kant is a philosopher who are Prussian." *These* kinds of grammatical mistakes will exhaust the patience of your reader and likely affect your grade.

22 Using a term vs. mentioning it

Sometimes we want to attribute a property to an object and sometimes we want to attribute a property to the word(s) that denote that object. Naturally, objects and the words that refer to them will have different properties. For example, the word "horse" has five letters but not four legs, whereas the horse who won the Belmont Stakes has four legs but not five letters. Some philosophers (W.V. Quine,[3] for example) think that grave mistakes have been made in the history of philosophy by failing to distinguish between properties of words and properties of objects, since some property may be a necessary feature of *how we refer to an object* although it is not a necessary feature of *the object itself.*

Explaining why the distinction between *using* a term to refer to an object and *mentioning* a word to talk about the word itself is an important one would take us too far afield for our present purposes; so, suffice it to say that you can avoid inadvertently entangling yourself in difficult issues in metaphysics and the theory of reference by observing the use/mention distinction in the following way. If you are mentioning a word in order to refer to it (for example, to say that the word has a property), then put quotation marks around the word. If you are using a word to perform its normal function, then write it as

---

[3] Quine (1908–2000) was one of the most important American philosophers of the twentieth century. Students can expect to encounter his essays in courses on the philosophy of language, logic, mathematics, epistemology, metaphysics, or Analytic Philosophy.

normal. You would want to write that whereas "horses" has six letters, horses have four legs (each).

Referring to concepts (as opposed to the words that name them) is a more tricky issue. When President Clinton said, "Freedom is expanding; for the first time in history, more than half the world's people elect their own leaders," he was referring to freedom – the capacity for individual self-determination (Clinton 1999). A statement such as "Freedom is related to truth," however, could either mean that (a) the concept of freedom will have whatever content it has because of certain logical relations it bears to the concept of truth or (b) there is no real-world freedom for individuals if those individuals are not afforded access to the truth. One way for an author to indicate that he or she is referring to the concept and not the state-of-affairs would be to write the word in quotation marks or italics. It is not always useful to put words referring to concepts in quotation marks or italics to distinguish them from the phenomena they capture, because usually it is clear from the context whether a concept or a phenomenon is being discussed. But, if there is any danger of confusion, put the word designating the concept in quotation marks or italics.

23 How to edit or add text within a quotation

Suppose you are writing about Descartes' claim that "this proposition, I am, I exist, is necessarily true whenever it is put forward by me or conceived in my mind" ([1641] 1985: 17). This proposition is usually glossed as "I think, therefore I am" and labeled "the *cogito*." If you were to write, "Descartes argues that he can identify a necessarily true proposition 'whenever it is put forward by me or conceived in my mind,'" it would be confusing. Your reader might be forced to ask, "Whenever *what* is put forward?" The problem is that the word "it" lost its referent in the new context. In the original text, "it" referred to the *cogito*. The confusion is easily remedied by replacing the word "it" with the bracketed amplification "[the *cogito*]." So instead of reading "whenever it is put forward . . ," the sentence will read "whenever [the *cogito*] is put forward . . ." Using square brackets within quotations tells the reader that the text appearing inside the brackets is supplied by you and not the writer you are quoting. Nonetheless, using square brackets to add text also implies that the amplification is nothing more than an accurate representation of the full meaning of the words that have been replaced.

Any time you change the text of a quotation (by cutting or adding words), you need to flag the change. If you cut something out, then use ellipses (i.e., ". . ."). If you have added italics to emphasize a word or phrase, then after citing the text and page, in parentheses write "emphasis added." Be careful whenever you alter the text that you are not changing the sense of the passage or inappropriately embellishing a passage to suit your purposes. This is a serious mistake that will ruin your paper and your grade. More importantly, it is intellectually dishonest to represent that a passage says one thing when the context indicates that it means something else.

Sometimes the text you are quoting contains a mistake in composition or printing. For a regular paper in one of your courses, if the mistake in the text is just a typographical error, you might just fix the mistake in the text and add a footnote explaining the mistake and your correction. However, if your paper is more formal – if it is intended to be scholarly or it will be published – then insert the signal "[sic]" after anything you think is an error in composition, editing, etc. However, do not remove the mistake. "Sic" means "thus" in Latin. It tells the reader that the original text reads *thus*, that you are not the cause of the error. You may tell the reader how you think the text should have read in your explanation of the passage or in a footnote. Sometimes commentators (especially indignant critics) will insert "[sic!]" after a statement or word-choice they find exasperating, but students do well to forgo the histrionics.

3.2 Elements of Substance

24 Avoid mere rhetoric: philosophy is not forensics

Writing philosophical papers requires careful, patient, and responsible thought and exposition. None of these virtues is prized or developed in most current forums of debate. Debates today are more likely to rely upon colorful examples or evocative language (i.e., what is disparagingly referred to as "purple prose") rather than genuine insight derived from the speaker's own knowledge.

Plato criticized the Sophists for employing rhetoric to persuade others in matters about which the Sophist himself had no real knowledge (1997a: 464b–466a). Suppose the Sophist is speaking on the topic of some proposed legislation the *justice* of which is in question. Since the Sophist has no knowledge of government, he cannot *explain* why the legislation is (or is not) just. Instead, the Sophist will only express what seems just, usually by pandering to the prejudices of the audience (1997b: 439a). That is to say, mere rhetoric is used to *persuade* when the author cannot *explain* through cogent argument. It is important to consider why Plato thought that using rhetoric to push conclusions whose truth one cannot explain is not just inaccurate but immoral.

Kant expressed a related view when he wrote in his *Lectures on Ethics*, "whatever militates against frankness lowers the dignity of man" (1980: 231; quoted in Korsgaard 1996: 142). And George Orwell wrote in "Politics and the English Language": "The great enemy of clear language is insincerity. When there is a gap between one's real and one's declared aims, one turns . . . instinctively to long words and exhausted idioms, like a cuttlefish squirting out ink" (1953: 167). Far from enticing the reader, the use of mere rhetoric in a philosophy paper – that is, any use of language with a purpose other than the clear, frank disclosure of the truth – will likely make your reader rightfully hostile toward your work.

Philosophers want to offer accounts and arguments that make a claim on our beliefs only insofar as we have considered the issues rationally. There is an important and neglected place for eloquence and elegance in writing and speaking. But if a choice has to be made, a philosopher will always take logical rigor and clarity over emotional or aesthetic appeal. Presumably, insofar as we want to be rational, we are obliged to give pride of place to valid argument and careful explication.

An even stronger claim for rational autonomy can be made. Suppose I am arguing for a particular thesis, and suppose you do not already agree with me. A champion of rational autonomy would say that you have a rational obligation *not* to accept what I am saying, unless I supply you with an argument whose premises you have good reason to believe and which provide some strong logical support for my thesis. This obligation stems, in part, from our duties to one another in the context of inquiry. I may be wrong in thinking that my thesis is correct. For example, I may believe premises that are false or draw conclusions that do not logically follow. Now, if you fail to hold me to the highest standards of proof, demonstration, and evidence, then an inadequate view will continue to exercise influence over how we think and act. And if you accept my thesis without going through the rigors of critical inquiry, then your beliefs will not only be less rational, but you will have sidelined one of the faculties the exercise of which makes us human.

25 Avoid using five-star vocabulary words

Although many students have spent an inordinate amount of time acquiring five-star words for college admissions tests, such words probably should not be used in philosophy papers. If you are certain that you have found the perfect word for what you intend to say, then by all means use it. However, you should always strive to make your point as directly and accessibly as possible.

Elsewhere in society, displaying an impressive vocabulary is one way to tell people that you went to fancy schools (or very much want to sound like someone who went to fancy schools). Philosophers could not care less about all that. We are happy to begin a conversation with the assumption that all the participants are equally entitled to have their views considered regardless of their credentials. All we care about is whether a person is capable of saying something insightful that illuminates an important problem. Displaying insight and using five-star words are not activities that usually go together, except on the part of essayists and experts.

Nevertheless, accessible and direct are not the same as untutored. Sometimes an uncommon word will, in fact, express more aptly what you mean to say. Cultivating your vocabulary, thus, enables you to express your mind accurately and artfully. However, just as you include only quotations or facts that advance your argument, you should only use terms and expressions that fit your subject matter and strategy. A philosophical audience will likely try to unpack your terminology to understand *everything* that is implied by the statements you make, the metaphors you use or the comparisons you draw. It can derail an otherwise promising paper to use an impressive term that, unfortunately, carries with it unhelpful or distracting associations.

26 The standard of precision in written discourse

Philosophers are simple folk, so try to use plain language. Using a thesaurus almost always results in word choice that is inaccurate, because people are typically drawn to words based on how they sound rather than what precisely they mean. In service of linguistic precision, buy the *Oxford English Dictionary* (which is what most academics use), and look up any remarkable words you are inclined to use, to make sure that they really do mean what you think they mean.

Take the example, "Plato proclaims . . ." If I may quote from the *OED*: "proclaim: Make official announcement of (something, that), esp. by word of mouth in a public place; cause this to be done by officers or agents; cause to become widely and publicly known; declare publicly (that)" (Brown 1993: 2365). Now, ask yourself: Did Plato really make an official and public announcement of his views? Doesn't the fact that Socrates (not Plato) is often the protagonist in literary dialogues (not expository essays) make this statement seem false simply as a matter of historical fact?

Not only is the use of this term unnecessary and odd, for a variety of philosophical texts – esoteric works (almost everything we have from Aristotle), heretical or politically dangerous views (almost everything written by Spinoza), and pseudonymous works (Kierkegaard) – writing that a philosopher "proclaims" his or her views would actually result in a historically false statement. Why not just write: "Plato writes . . . ," "Plato holds . . . ," or (perhaps better) "Socrates argues that . . ."? In philosophy, the world hangs on your choice of terms, their meaning, and their inferential relations to other terms. Since the meaning and logical import of any two words will likely be different, it is crucial that you say *exactly* what your argument, the text or the facts permit you to say.

27 On expressions such as "It is clear that . . ."

Do not write, "It is clear that . . ." That is just rhetoric. If it were so clear, you probably would not be talking about it. It is the writer's job to *make* a statement clear, not to *tell* the reader that something is clear.

A similar danger exists (flagged above in ℓ 10) whenever you use conclusion indicators – those words or expressions signaling to the reader that your line of reasoning leads to the statement that follows. If a paragraph in your paper consists of three sentences and the first two are premises of an argument, then by all means begin the third and last sentence with a conclusion indicator such as "It follows that . . ." and then state the conclusion. However, if you write "It follows that . . ." without having given your reader adequate reasons to accept the statement that follows, then you have made a *conclusory statement* and not a legitimate use of a conclusion indicator. It is mere rhetoric to write "Consequently . . ." or "It follows that . . ." where the statement that follows is not logically implied by what precedes it.

Given that it is sometimes difficult to tell whether an author has supplied the reader with adequate reasons to accept a conclusion, you should offer an explanation of the inferences you make (and those that you urge the reader to make), rather than merely state them. If your premises logically imply your conclusion, then show us why the conclusion has to be true whenever the premises are true. It will enhance your credibility with the reader if you avoid conclusory statements and explain your inferences. Doing so shows that you respect your reader's intelligence and that the purpose of your paper is to develop your arguments, rather than to pursue an ideological objective.

28 Use accurate terms having clear referents

If you refer to all members of "the human family" (as the preamble to the *Universal Declaration of Human Rights* [1948] does), your instructor might write in the margin, "What on earth is that?" and perhaps will ask "Have you given me any reason to think that there is such a thing?" If you are referring to the species, then say that. If you are referring to the nations that are subject to international law, then say that. If you are discussing a religious view, and you are referring to all things created in the image of God (leaving aside what that might mean), then say that. In philosophy, it is almost impossible to slip theoretical indecision past your reader by using imprecise terminology, where it is unclear to what *exactly* the term is supposed to refer. As you read through your paper, ask yourself: "Would anyone who can read English have a clear idea what I am talking about here?"

If the answer is "No," then either choose a different term or explain what you mean.

29 Always look for the contrast term

A reader who encountered an expression such as "good virtues" might well ask him- or herself, "As opposed to what – *bad* virtues?" The word "good" does not add anything here because it does not rule anything out. The class of virtues and the class of good virtues are the same class. If you cannot think of what contrasts with a term you have used, it probably means nothing and you should choose a different term.

30 Watch out for mysterious agents

The sentence "Natural rights protect the well-being of citizens" makes a strange claim. An abstract object is doing something rather concrete. Is it not, rather, that when a government protects natural rights, it thereby protects the well-being of its citizens? The next step in saying something specific is to spell out what it means for governments to protect natural rights, but you see where I am going with this. Make sure that you are committed even to the claims you are making *implicitly*.

3.3 Substantive Advice

31 Never quote the instructor

An interpretation is justified only if it is adequate to the text. So the fact that the instructor claimed that Aristotle means such-and-such in some passage does not carry any weight by itself in a paper. The instructor probably developed an interpretation that was supported by many passages and made sense out of many passages. And the claim about what Aristotle meant was supported by that interpretive work. You need to do the same kind of interpretive work in your paper.

Also, instructors rarely recognize themselves when their lectures are "quoted" in their students' papers. It is quite likely that when you write, "As Professor Z said in class . . ." the professor will either think "Well, that student sure wasn't listening . . ." (if you didn't understand him or her) or "Why isn't the student doing the arguing and interpreting for himself?" (if you did). You really cannot win. Take your instructors' lectures as commentaries on and contributions to a debate. They should help orient *your own* reading and research. And the paper you turn in should argue for a thesis that is supported by your own reading and research.

32 Never quote the dictionary

Philosophers do not care what *Webster's* or even the *Oxford English Dictionary* has for a definition of "duty." If you are writing on Kant, we want to know what Kant meant by "duty." If you substitute *Webster's* definition for Kant's, then you will end up perverting Kant's views.

Dictionaries record the meaning that a word currently has in a linguistic community. They have no greater authority than that. If Kant meant something that is not within *Webster's* definition, this does not mean that Kant is wrong or that he has neglected something. Philosophy sometimes helps us to understand better the terms we employ by showing us how they are related to other terms; sometimes it shows that a term is inadequate to the phenomena it is supposed to capture; sometimes it shows us that a term has evolved or been obscured or co-opted. If you simply rest content with what the dictionary says "duty" is, then you will only know what your neighbors mean by the term, but nothing more intellectually, historically or morally significant.

3.4 A Few Frequently Misused Terms

33 Philosophy vs. view vs. opinion

An opinion is a belief that one is not prepared to justify to another if challenged. I think that Bach's cello sonatas are fabulous; but if you do not, then well (I may say to myself) there is no accounting for taste. But I also think that the standard account of logical consequence is inadequate. Now, *this belief* I am prepared to defend; and, in fact, I did defend it at length in my dissertation. In short, it is not just my *opinion* that the standard account of logical consequence is wrong. It is more accurate to say that it is my *view*, or if my view is part of an alternative account, you might call it my *account*. This is not to say that opinions pertain to things that are subjective or that someone only holds a view if he or she is right. The distinguishing characteristic is whether a person has gone to the trouble of making his or her commitments responsive to reasons. Alternatively, although I hold a view about the standard account of logical consequence, it would be inaccurate to say that I had developed a *philosophy* of logic. I have not, because I have no relatively comprehensive network of well-reasoned, mutually-consistent, and similarly-motivated and -justified views on the major questions concerning logic.

34 Concept vs. conception

Usually when philosophers use the term "concept," they are simply referring to whatever it is in terms of which we think. We think *about* things, and whatever mental representations or mental categories we use to do that are called "concepts." There is a rich literature in the philosophy of mind on concepts – what they are, how they fit into physical explanations of the brain, how they relate to linguistic units such as propositions or words – but we all (including philosophers) talk about concepts without necessarily intending to take a position on these contested questions in the philosophy of mind. When we focus on a concept rather than the real-world phenomena it picks out – for example, the concept of "mother" rather than any of the specific women who are or have been mothers – we often do so to ask criterial questions ("Who counts as a mother and why?") or to explore what other properties are logically implied by the concept ("Do some women have special moral duties just in virtue of being mothers?").

Conceptions are the working-out of concepts. That is to say, philosophers use the word "conception" to refer to an account of how a concept is properly applied in a given context. The *concept* of knowledge may be developed into a *conception* of how we might come to know something on the basis of someone's testimony. Such a conception might hold that the testimony of one gives rise to knowledge for others only if the witness knows the proposition she reported, we understand the proposition, and we know that the information was reliably conveyed by the witness. A philosopher who develops such an account contributes a *conception* of knowledge to the epistemology of testimony. Conceptions build out from concepts and concepts may derive their content (at least in part) from their place within the conceptions in which the concepts are developed and applied.[4]

35 Think vs. feel

I *feel* that people are not kind enough to one another. That is to say, it makes me *sad* to see people be mean; I am *hopeful* that people will change; I am *encouraged* when I see acts of kindness; etc. Emotions are wonderful and important things. In fact, it is appropriate (contrary to what your high school teachers may have told you) to write about your emotions in academic work. One acceptable use of "feel" is when one writes: "I feel that such-and-such is important because . . ." Furthermore, philosophers (for better of worse) routinely appeal to our "intuitions" to test conceptions for plausibility. And there is no good reason why emotions should not be considered members in good standing of our set of intuitions, especially when value judgments are at issue.

Nevertheless, it is false to say: "I *feel* that Plato's metaphysics provides an adequate account of predication and existential propositions." I have no feelings about it one way or the other. I have *thoughts* about it, because Michael Frede[5] has written on it and I have read some of his work. I *understand* a little, but I do not understand it all. I *follow* some arguments, but I do not follow all of them. The mental events that occur to me pertaining to Plato's metaphysics are entirely *cognitive* events. Not one of them is an emotion.[6] Usually when we take up a position in a philosophy paper – reporting as to whether we agree

---

[4] I think the foregoing discussion agrees in its essentials with Ronald Dworkin's explanation of the distinction between concept and conception in *Law's Empire* (1986: 70–1), although I do not agree that the distinction is between "different levels of abstraction."

[5] Frede (1940–2007) taught at Oxford University, where he held the Chair in the History of Philosophy. He wrote primarily on ancient and Hellenistic philosophy.

[6] Actually, I do have a few emotions about Frede's work on Plato. However, although my shrink may be interested in the fact that I am *happy* that Frede had such interesting thoughts and that I get *depressed* because I am not as smart as he, there is no reason to talk about any of this in a philosophy paper.

or disagree, have been persuaded or remain doubtful, for example – we are reporting a cognitive event. So be sure to use the appropriate verb to refer to the sort of mental event you have had.

36 Statement vs. argument

It is not Kant's *argument* that the only thing that is good, properly so-called, is a will directed by duty. This is a statement that Kant would endorse (if I have understood him correctly). And he has an argument for it. But a statement is not an argument. An argument consists of at least two sentences, at least one of which is a premise, and at most one of which is the conclusion; and the premises provide some reason for accepting the conclusion as true. A statement is an expression of a sentence. It is the sort of thing that is true or false, not valid or invalid. Furthermore, it is incorrect to write: "Kant's argument is, Should not happiness and virtue eventually be commensurate?" Kant may have asked that question, made a statement in answer to it, and then given an argument for that statement. But just as an argument is not a statement, it certainly is not a question.

37 Sound, valid, and true

To be *sound* in philosophy means to be a valid argument with true premises. Thus, views are not sound, and neither are statements. To be *valid* in philosophy means to be an argument with premises that, if true, necessitate the truth of the conclusion. Arguments are not true or false. To be *true* in philosophy is – well, there is no consensus on this, really. It is a property (if indeed it is a property) either of thoughts, propositions, sentences, or utterances. And (just to mention one option) sentences or thoughts are true if they correctly represent the facts.

4

Explaining Philosophical Texts

¶ 38 Make sense out of the text as a whole

If you are interpreting some single part of a philosopher's text, then you ought to be cognizant of the rest of the text. That does not mean that you have to write about it. Your awareness of the rest of the text – other arguments the author makes, other premises the author invokes, other criticisms the author offers – may perfectly well stay in the background as you develop your own argument. Still, the understanding of the *specific* passages that you develop and defend in your paper ought to be consistent with your *general* understanding of the tenor of the text as a coherent piece of philosophical writing.

You may think, nonetheless, that a philosopher's article or book is *not* a coherent piece of philosophical writing. And you may be right. This is not all that uncommon. Of course, you should first satisfy yourself that you have interpreted the text charitably (see ¶ 3). Only attribute incoherence to a piece of philosophical writing if the plain language of the text forces you to diagnose irreconcilable tension. Sometimes the appearance of tension between two statements vanishes once you have reached a firmer grasp of what they *individually* mean within the *general* context of the philosophical project carried out in the text.

There is something called the *hermeneutic circle* that is useful to keep in mind when doing philosophy. Your understanding of a specific passage depends on your prior hypothesis (some would call it a *pre-conception*) about the purpose and meaning of the whole text. It would be impossible to take a statement *as a premise* unless you came to the text believing that it would be possible to find an argument in it. For example, you would probably not interpret a line in a book of poetry as a premise, because poems tend not to be arguments. And we are generally unable to understand the concepts employed in a given statement unless we can place the sentence in a broader context. For example, we would not know how to understand the concept of knowledge in a particular philosophical text unless we had *some* underlying supposition about the philosopher's view of the mind and its relationship to facts. Our understanding of a particular passage is oriented around a prior understanding of the nature of the text as a whole.

Conversely, your supposition as to the meaning of the whole will have to be supported by, or revised in light of, your interpretation of the constituent parts. Suppose you began reading René Descartes[1] with the understanding that he was a materialist, that is, one who believes that everything that exists is physical, located in space and time. Suppose you encountered the following passage in Descartes' work *The Passions of the Soul*: "And the soul is of such a nature that it has no relation to extension, or to the dimensions or other properties of the matter of which the body is composed . . ." ([1649] 1985: 339). Your global presupposition about Descartes's approach to philosophy has to be revised in light of your interpretation of this passage, because this passage stands in direct contradiction to your preconception of Descartes' metaphysics.

The relevance of the hermeneutic circle to philosophical writing is that your interpretation of those passages you plan to discuss will depend on your interpretation of the text as a whole; and your broader interpretation of the text will sometimes be confirmed and sometimes undermined by your understanding of individual passages. A good philosophy paper will propose interpretations of passages that are permitted by a reasonable interpretation of the whole text and interpretations of the whole text that are informed by accurate readings of specific passages.

---

[1] Descartes (1596–1650) developed analytical geometry, worked in optics, and initiated the Modern era in philosophy, most famously with his *Meditations on First Philosophy* (1641). Students can expect to read Descartes in courses in Modern Philosophy (or, more specifically, Continental Rationalism) and epistemology.

39 Make sense out of the main arguments in a text

Lawyers make a very helpful distinction between the *holding* of a court in a case and *obiter dicta* that occur in the written opinion. The *holding* is the legal rule announced or applied that is *essential* to the court's decision in a particular case. For example, as is familiar from movies and television, part of the holding of the case *Miranda v. Arizona* is:

> [I]f a person in [police] custody is to be subject to interrogation, he must first be informed in clear and unequivocal terms that he has the right to remain silent. The warning of the right to remain silent must be accompanied by the explanation that anything said can and will be used against the individual in court . . . In order fully to apprise a person interrogated of the extent of his rights, it is necessary to warn him not only that he has the right to consult with an attorney, but also that if he is indigent a lawyer will be appointed to represent him." (*Miranda v. Arizona* 1966: 467–8, 473)

Obiter dicta (or just "*dicta*") are all the other interesting and valuable but not legally-essential statements of the judge(s) that signed the opinion. *Dicta* have little legal authority, whereas holdings become part of the law within the jurisdiction of the court.

If, by analogy, we apply the holding/*dicta* distinction to philosophical texts, the "holding" of a text is the argument the philosopher offers to address a given problem. The "*dicta*" of a text are all of the other interesting things the philosopher happens to think about related or unrelated topics. If the author is trying to answer a question, then the "holding" will include the author's argument (premises and conclusion) for his or her answer, any justification the author offers for accepting the premises, and the explanation for why he or she has posed the problem in the particular way he or she did. These elements of the text define the author's rational accomplishment and will become known as the author's view or position on the matter. The "*dicta*" in a philosophical text will consist of all the other comments – no matter how profound or eloquent – that are not logically essential to the philosopher's defense of his or her thesis. The elements of an author's main argument identified above are meant to be illustrative, not exhaustive. It would be silly to think that a simple formula could be used to separate the main argument from less important commentary across all authors and all philosophical texts. You must be sensitive to the specific text and author you are considering in order to tease apart the main lines of an argument from possibly illuminating but ultimately inessential commentary.

"*Dicta*" in philosophical texts can offer fantastic clues about how to interpret the text in which they appear or other texts by the same author. They can be of great biographical and historical interest. They might help you to find the most charitable understanding of the philosopher's project. And they may have some bearing on arguments the author makes elsewhere. But if you have set out to understand and interpret a specific text, it is generally a mistake to take one or two remarks from that text that are not part of the central argument and make them the primary focus of your analysis.[2] If you do so, your instructor will think that you failed either to grasp the main thrust of that text or to grapple with the central issues set out therein.

"*Dicta*" can be tempting targets for philosophy papers because they tend to be more colorful (that is, controversial or outrageous) than the carefully-stated parts of the philosopher's "holding." But, for the purposes of most undergraduate philosophy papers, it is better to demonstrate in your paper that you have grasped the main arguments of the text under consideration, rather than to launch into an analysis of one of the author's minor tangents.

40 Every quotation requires explanation

Very few passages in philosophical works have a meaning or import that is transparently clear. Almost every passage you are likely to quote will require explanation, no matter how obvious the meaning and

---

[2] Of course, some philosophers have written interesting books by focusing on a sentence of some author that is not obviously related to an argument and using it to gain some insight into other things the author has written. Jacques Derrida's (1981) *Spurs: Nietzsche's Style's*, comes to mind, in which Friedrich Nietzsche's seemingly irrelevant "I have forgotten my umbrella" is used to "decode" Nietzsche's view of truth (among other things). Psychoanalytically-inclined philosophers might employ a parallel method by viewing a writer's asides as clues to the underlying structure of the writer's project. But, *in general*, such projects are decidedly *not* what instructors are looking for in undergraduate philosophy papers.

significance of the passage is to you. For this reason, you should rarely end a paragraph with a quotation.

If you are writing a paper that is primarily interpretive, and you need to evaluate the merits of rival interpretations of a passage (or even a single word), then you must quote the passage *and parse it out*. Naked quotations without explanation only show that a particular passage happens to appear in some philosopher's text. But if a quotation is supposed to be evidence supporting your view, then you need to explain the import of the passage and, thereby, argue for the merits of your interpretation. Thus, the guiding voice in your paper must be your own, not that of the author you are quoting.

For the foregoing reasons, you should give careful consideration to whether a quotation is really necessary or whether, instead, a faithful paraphrase is sufficient to join issue with the author and move ahead with your argument. The answer to this question is often determined by which of the following is your strategy: (a) to convey that the author made a particular argument, conveyed an idea, developed a view, took a position, etc.; or (b) to demonstrate that an author used specific words, employed particular rhetoric, made certain specific connections, relied on intricate and subtle inferences, etc. All too often, commentators take liberties in paraphrasing an author's text, such that the ensuing discussion is irrelevant and unfair to the arguments the author actually made. For this reason, quoting and explaining is good discipline for those whose business it is to make sound arguments. But it is equally good discipline to put into your own words an accurate restatement of someone else's ideas. And, especially for papers that are more argument-driven than text-driven – i.e., more (a) than (b), above – you will be able to address your objective more directly and efficiently if you paraphrase your interlocutors rather than quote them.

Never begin an explanation of a quotation with "Meaning that . . ." or "Implying that . . ." It is next to impossible to end up with a grammatical sentence of English if you begin with those words.

41 Every quotation requires specific attribution

If you quote a philosopher, then you must tell the reader where he or she can find that passage. This means that you have to tell the reader the specific publication information, including edition, and the page on which to find it. Remember that you are writing in order to bring the reader to exactly the same conclusion that you have reached. Presumably you have come to this conclusion through a very specific consideration of the texts and arguments. One way to think about writing a paper is that you are trying to take the reader through the considerations that led you to your conclusion. In order to do this, the reader has to be able to find the passages you think are important enough to mention in your paper so that he or she can consider them afresh, in light of your interpretation.

Most philosophy teachers I have studied under do not care which particular convention of citation was used. I think the reason for this is that the only time it will really matter whether you have followed a citation style exactly is if you are publishing, and each journal or press has its own citation style that you will have to follow. So it does not do much good to internalize a particular style, since you will have to change things around anyway when it counts.

The Vancouver and Harvard systems are probably the most common styles of citation, although style manuals generally supply others. One style of citation for articles, chapters, and books (respectively) that is based on the Harvard system looks like this:

Mogck, B.D. (2002a) Some Pretty Good Ideas. *Journal Title* Volume ## (issue ##): ##–##.
Mogck, B.D. (2002b) Profound Thoughts? In: Chamberlin, J.C., Elving, J.J., & Schnell, R.L. (eds.), *Lots of Profound Thoughts.* City of Publication: Press, pp. ##–##.
Mogck, B.D. (2002c) *Why Hutchens' Logical Theory is Wrong.* City of publication: Press.

This style permits one to include the original reference in a footnote or reference page, and make parenthetical reference in the text either by writing "[end of sentence] (Mogck 2002a: 58) [punctuation]" or by writing "Mogck argues in (2002c). . . ." Only use lower-case letters after the year if you are citing more than one text by the same author(s) published in the same year; otherwise, just use the year. If a text was translated from one language to the language of the text you are citing, then immediately after the title of the translated text add a comma and write "trans. So-and-so." (For further discussion of proper attribution, see Chapter 6).

℘ 42 The consistent and meaningful use of technical terminology

WHAT IS TECHNICAL TERMINOLOGY?

In almost every philosophical text, there will be terms that have a special significance to the philosopher you are explaining or the argument you are making. For example, "nature" in Aristotle's philosophy has a special meaning that is distinct from what most people living today would mean by using "nature." "Idea" has the same status in Plato's philosophy. "Clear" and "distinct" are examples from Descartes. If you have understood the philosopher you are explaining, then you will know which terms carry a special meaning in his or her philosophy. Any terms that carry specific meaning in the texts you are explaining are "technical terms." Also, if anything important rides on a philosopher having used a particular term or avoided a particular term, then that term is also being used (or avoided) "technically".

It is essential that you explain what you think the philosopher means by his or her technical terminology. This is important because defining the terminology is an indispensable part of explaining what you are talking about, and making clear to your reader that you have understood the text. It is also a helpful way to get on the same page with your reader, since before reading your paper it is likely that your reader had a slightly different appreciation of the terminology and its meaning than the one you are assuming or advocating.

ONCE YOU HAVE DEFINED YOUR TERMS, USE THEM CONSISTENTLY

Be very careful when you quote a philosopher's definition of a technical term and then write, "This means that . . ." Even though sentences that explain what a term means may not *seem* like they would be among the most important or controversial in a paper, they can be. So make sure that your elaborations are accurate and supported not only by the passages you are quoting but by other passages containing the term as well. Finally, the definition you offer of a technical term must, for the sake of consistency, be observed in your explanation of any quotation in which the technical term occurs.

5

The Rudiments of Academic Research

43 Use the library, not the Web

The Web provides an amazing array of tools to use in exploring a field such as philosophy. Philosophers may use it to keep up-to-date with what is being taught at universities around the world, what has just been published in their areas of research, and what online resources may be of use to their students or themselves.

That being said, the use of the Web to *do* research in philosophy today is a *serious* mistake. First, students forgo the chance to learn how to do primary source, library research – a crucial skill no matter what their professional goals. Second, the quality of online resources is often quite dubious. There is no process of peer review[1] or editorial supervision to help ensure that what is "published" on the Web has significant merit.[2] Wikipedia is the *cause célèbre* for this misgiving.

Given that so many sites and links are either dead or useless, ten minutes with a book in the library would likely be more productive

---

[1] Peer review is the process whereby an article or a book submitted for publication is scrutinized by a panel of experts to ensure that the work complies with the scientific and/or scholarly standards of the field. It is an invaluable quality-control mechanism that enables non-experts to have a high degree of confidence in the value of certain publications.

[2] I would especially recommend against paying any attention to philosophy message boards, which often contain the confused musings of nonprofessionals or the technical minutiae of professionals, neither of which will be of any service to most undergraduates (or most anyone else).

than an hour surfing the Web. Third, far too often students (knowingly or not) plagiarize online resources by "picking up" ideas or cutting and pasting passages without proper attribution. The informality and speed of the Internet make it all too easy to commit this offense. Students who rely on quick-and-dirty searches miss an opportunity to come to a firm grasp of the conceptual and literary landscape through good old-fashioned reading and reflection. This leads into my fourth misgiving. A liberal arts education ought to produce highly-literate, sophisticated thinkers. Yet, the prevailing manner of Web use by students today (rapid browsing and copying) is antithetical to this goal.

For this reason I recommend the following policy: sources cited in papers should, as a rule, be published on paper, even if they are made available to students to read online. Sources that are published in the first instance online are acceptable only if they are peer-reviewed.[3] Aside from peer-reviewed, scholarly publications, the Web might be consulted for leads and references, but should not be considered a primary or secondary source for research. Even if a website appears to contain the entire text of one of the primary sources in your class – for example, if it appears to reproduce the entire text of Plato's dialogue *The Apology* – websites are often full of mistakes and should not be assumed to be reliable. Several of the online texts I have come across are draft versions of the published edition that contain inaccuracies and, for that reason, are not authoritative. The Web is a research tool. That is to say, it should be used to *facilitate* research that accords with the professional standards of the discipline. In philosophy, the professional standards do not currently permit *conducting* research on the Web.

The use of authorized e-texts that are made available through your university library is different, because these meet both the publication and peer review requirements mentioned above. However, a word of

---

[3]   The website of the main professional association for philosophers in the United States, The American Philosophical Association, has a list of online journals available at <http://www.apa.udel.edu/apa/asp/journals.asp>. You may follow these links, and check with each journal to see if it is peer reviewed. Several of the links I followed indicated that subscriptions to the journals were necessary to read their contents; so, again, why not just go to the library where you know you will be able to read the article once you have found it?

caution is in order. The use of searchable e-texts can be dangerous if, instead of reading the book, you merely read those sentences in which a particular keyword occurs. You should search the text to see which larger units of expression (chapters, for example) contain discussion of the term that interests you, and then read the entire unit. Only then will you understand the role of the term in the author's argument.

There are two good resources that students might find useful and which I think it would be acceptable to cite (but check with your instructor first):

1 The *Stanford Encyclopedia of Philosophy*, available at <http://plato. stanford.edu/>; and
2 The Perseus Digital Library (which contains searchable ancient and medieval texts), available at <http://www.perseus.tufts.edu/>.

I would also recommend the following sites that contain mostly reliable information, but which also contain some informal or provisional material that it might be inappropriate to cite:

3 *Ethics Updates*, hosted by Lawrence Hinman of the University of San Diego, available at <http://ethics.sandiego.edu/>; and
4 The Internet Encyclopedia of Philosophy, available at <http://www.utm.edu/research/iep/>.

44 Primary sources are your primary responsibility

It is important to focus in your papers and exams on the assigned materials. And it is important that you invest the majority of your effort understanding the philosopher's text rather than the text of a commentator. A "primary source" is a text that is considered an important work of philosophy, whereas a "secondary source" is *a study of* a primary source. Sometimes secondary sources are so original and insightful that they become primary sources in their own right. Nonetheless, secondary sources are usually not the primary focus of undergraduate philosophy courses. So even if a secondary source has been helpful in your study of a text, you will generally be expected to grapple with and spill the majority of ink explaining primary sources.

45 What kind of secondary sources should be used and how?

Students can benefit, in the first instance, from reading secondary sources in order to gain an understanding of the context or main lines of a book or a philosopher's thought. Later, once you have worked hard to develop your own interpretation of a text, a secondary source may provide helpful counterpoint and dialogue, encouraging you to further refine your arguments or consider some new objections. Secondary sources can also help to put you on the right track as you prepare to write a paper. For example, you might not know where in Plato's corpus to find a discussion of courage, but perhaps a book on Plato's political theory will tell you. Or you might begin to develop your own view on Plato's political theory by showing where another commentator's view is wrong or, even if it is right, inadequately justified or underdeveloped.

Students can also benefit by using reference books in philosophy to understand some piece of technical jargon (e.g., "contextualism" in epistemology or "deontology" in ethics or "anti-realism" in metaphysics). In this regard, students might consult *The Cambridge Dictionary of Philosophy* (Audi 1995), *The Routledge Encyclopedia of Philosophy* (Craig 1998), or the *Stanford Encyclopedia of Philosophy* (Zalta 2007). Reading the explanations and definitions found in reference texts such as these often helps students become oriented in the discipline. Nevertheless, in general, you should not primarily engage with an encyclopedia or dictionary of philosophy in a paper. You should, instead, grapple with primary sources.[4] But it is appropriate to express an intellectual debt or mention a reference text in one's "Works Consulted" section. Your instructor selected particular texts for you to study and explain in your papers. If your explanation of these texts requires a definition or explanation, you should glean one from the text itself, rather than from a reference text.

The most important reason that students might read secondary sources is that secondary sources give students a tangible example of what they should aim to produce in their papers. Instructions like

---

[4] There are, of course, exceptions. But they probably only apply to advanced graduate students and professionals, so I will not mention them.

those canvassed in this book only go so far. Role models are just as important in writing as they are in the rest of life. If you want to *write* good papers, then you have to *read* good papers. I once wrote a paper on Kant, whose works are often painfully difficult to read, and the professor made a devastating criticism of my paper: he said I wrote like Kant! But, if that is all you have ever seen in philosophy, then that is what you will produce (much to everyone's dismay).

Nevertheless, keep in mind that your focus should not shift away from the primary sources. You must understand the author on his or her own terms. You must not rely on a commentator on Kant to avoid doing the difficult work of reading Kant for yourself. It is unacceptable and inaccurate to write "As Kant says . . ." and then quote a commentator. If you want to claim that Kant is committed to some claim, then you need to show this by working through his text. Why would the instructor reward you with a good grade for reproducing what someone else went to the trouble of demonstrating? Consulting a secondary source can facilitate textual interpretation, but must not replace it.

One thing that undergraduates should know is that many philosophers writing in English from the twentieth century forward write articles more often than they write books. Thus, library research for recent scholarship will require looking for journal articles in addition to monographs.

To find articles, students should consult *The Philosopher's Index* or *JSTOR*, which are searchable databases to which your library might subscribe. However, because they contain mostly scholarly debate that is not usually worth unraveling for the purposes of most undergraduate papers, they are more appropriate for students working on major research papers (such as a senior seminar paper or an honors thesis), rather than an ordinary term paper. In general, simply ask your instructor to recommend a good article or at least a good author for the topic of your paper. This will save you a lot of needless effort sifting through search results. Consulting first with your instructor will also hopefully forefend against the hazard of choosing a commentator whom your instructor hates. It is rather disconcerting to invest valuable time reading a secondary source only to have your instructor comment: "But that commentator is a hack and a moron!"

Part II

Doing Philosophy

6

Academic Integrity

6.1 Know Your School's Honor Code and its Policies Regarding Plagiarism

Many students do not know whether their school has an Honor Code or, if it does, what it says. Ignorance carries with it certain dangers; and students run the risk of serious heartaches by ignoring rules that, if violated, can result in a failing grade or even expulsion. Ignorance of the law is no defense outside of academia, and it does not work inside academia either. Self-preservation and moral responsibility counsel in favor of students familiarizing themselves with the governing Honor Code. They ought to do this, obviously, *before* submitting any papers or exams.

6.2 What is Plagiarism?

Because many students do not know what plagiarism is, warning against it tends to be rather ineffective. It is the prerogative of your school to define plagiarism. And if the school has not done that, then it is the prerogative of your instructors. However, just to help orient you to the basic concerns, I offer a provisional definition.

A student commits plagiarism if the work he or she submits for a course either: (a) is not his or her own original research and writing, prepared by the student specifically for that course; or (b) contains any use, mention, reproduction, or influence of another person's work within his or her own work without proper attribution. By "proper attribution" I mean at a minimum the use of quotation marks to indicate direct quotations and proper citation to the source of any influence.[1] Some examples of plagiarism include:

- ☑ submitting a paper (or some part thereof) that you prepared and submitted for a different class;
- ☑ submitting a paper (of some part thereof) that someone else wrote;
- ☑ using the language or content of another paper to form the substance of your own, no matter how extensively you modify or paraphrase the material;
- ☑ using the argument, explanation, data, or research of another author and presenting it without proper attribution as your own original work; and
- ☑ quoting anything without using quotation marks and proper attribution.

Although a student who plagiarizes an entire paper is guilty of a greater offense against academic integrity than a student who plagiarizes a single sentence or argument, "no plagiarist can excuse the wrong by showing how much of his work he did not pirate" (*Sheldon* v. *Metro-Goldwyn Pictures Corp.* 1936: 56).

6.3 How to Avoid Plagiarism

A useful rule of thumb is as follows: if you found an idea in or thought one up while reading another text, or you heard about an idea from or was told about it by anybody (however informal), then make that influence explicit in your references section or in a footnote. It probably does not matter which convention of citation you use, so long as you use it consistently and employ it wherever academic honesty dictates. Common citation conventions can be found in most any style manual, such as *The Chicago Manual of Style*. I give a few examples based on the Harvard system in ℓ 41. However, it probably would suffice just to look at how sources are cited in your textbooks and follow that style.

---

[1] For further discussion of proper attribution, see ℓ 41.

6.4 Proper Attribution Bolsters One's Scholarly Credibility

Students often do not attribute appropriately out of a concern that their own voices will be lost amidst all the references and acknowledgments of influence. What they perhaps do not fully appreciate is that part of the purpose of their academic work is to demonstrate that they are competent participants in a larger discussion. One of the ways that students can demonstrate their competence is to show that they: (a) are familiar with the major texts and figures in a debate; and, (b) have read and been influenced by these encounters. Far from diminishing a student's voice, proper citation and attribution is a precondition for the credibility and scholarly value of their contribution. It is, of course, also expected that students will make an original contribution in their academic work, however modest or tentative.

6.5 Cheaters are Likely to be Caught

Even instructors who are overwhelmed with their teaching and research responsibilities often catch cheating. Give your instructors a little credit. They have seen hundreds if not thousands of examples of the sort of assignment you are asked to complete. They know what to expect of their students – even exceptional students (because they have had those before too!)

Taking materials from the Internet is just plain stupid. Professors can Google™ with the best of them. After I noticed that one student's paper was a little *too* scholarly and polished to have been written by an undergraduate in a few weeks, it took me all of about 30 seconds to find the exact website from which the paper was lifted. (And, no, paraphrasing will not solve the problem, because keyword searches will turn up the same materials.) Some universities are turning to electronic services that allow instructors to search students' papers for plagiarized material. There are even programs that allow instructors to check to see if any of the material in a paper comes from an online paper mill.

Even more basically, think how unlikely it is that you would hand in a paper that would fit in with what the rest of your classmates produced if it was written by someone who did not read exactly the same assigned texts, was not part of the same class discussions, did not hear the same lectures, and did not have exactly the same assignment. So, although I would hope that the moral argument would be persuasive enough – you should never cheat because it is dishonest – prudence counsels against plagiarism as well.

7

How to Succeed in
a Philosophy Course

7.1 Practice the Intellectual Virtues

7.1.1 Curiosity

It is important that students have a desire to learn about themselves, the world in which they live, and the history of the traditions in which they participate. Students who have focused very early on a pre-professional track (pre-med, pre-law, pre-business) sometimes have little patience for these cornerstones of a liberal arts education. That is too bad. If they were to talk to scientists, doctors, lawyers, and successful business people, they would find that a critical and thoughtful understanding of human values is an incredibly valuable asset and often a professional necessity. Philosophers have often urged that there is a moral issue here as well: by trying to justify our beliefs and practices we will: (a) hold fewer false beliefs; (b) conduct ourselves more rationally; and (c) conduct ourselves more justly. One contemporary philosopher (Nussbaum 1998) has referred to education as the cultivation of our very humanity, following the Roman Stoic Seneca.

Of course, it is a contradiction in terms to *enforce* curiosity, so there is something radically *optional* about reading philosophy for the purpose of cultivating your humanity. The right response to someone who wonders why he or she *ought* to do philosophy was given by Robert Penn Warren in response to the question why someone *ought* to read the great writer of the American South, William Faulkner:

I don't know why a person *should* read anything . . . I mean maybe we're doomed to a world in which nobody will read . . . Maybe we're doomed to be animals and go back to the caves. I think a person who wants to be human should read Faulkner. Now, if you're satisfied with your degree of humanity and your understanding of human nature, don't read him. But if you have any discontent or any aspiration to be more human than you are, read him. (Levinger 2000: 80)

Likewise, the "aspiration to be more human than you are" sparks the curiosity that ignites philosophical questioning.

7.1.2 Humility

It is important for those studying philosophy to admit that they are asking difficult questions and reading difficult texts in which the authors struggled with similar difficult questions. Sometimes the questions raised in philosophical texts concern the reasons we have for holding our most fundamental commitments. These questions may not have occurred to you before taking a philosophy course. Or perhaps they have, but you were discouraged from pursuing them. Or perhaps you just did not know how to begin thinking them through. Other times, the questions raised in philosophical texts are difficult to ask because the concepts and methods involved are not well-understood. What, after all, is our concept of God? Is it immediately clear to what we are committed if we believe that God *exists*? Does philosophy have a specific (set of) method(s), distinct from the natural and social sciences but also from religion, which philosophers use to answer these questions? These are important issues to address. But it will require patient reading, writing, and discussion to answer them intelligently. Students do well to keep in mind the following:

1 There are important questions that you have already considered. Remember that other smart people have considered these questions too. Your inquiry can benefit from their insights and mistakes. Conversely, their inquiries and those of your contemporaries may benefit from your insights and mistakes. Thus, developing a well-considered view will qualify you as a valued participant in the conversation.

2   There are important questions that you may not yet have considered. These questions may be vital and ought not to be ignored just because they are unfamiliar. Likewise, just because you are a thoughtful and intelligent person does not mean that you will have an answer to every important question. As Saul Bellow wrote in *Herzog*, "Readiness to answer all questions is the infallible sign of stupidity" ([1964] 1996: 155).

3   There are beliefs that are important to you that you may not yet be prepared to defend with adequate reasons. It is important to stress that this is true of everyone, Nobel laureates included. Philosophers are in the business of testing and improving upon the justifications we have for holding our beliefs. They follow Mill in holding that, "[i]f the cultivation of the understanding consists in one thing more than in another, it is surely in learning the grounds of one's own opinions" ([1859] 1989: 37).

4   Philosophical texts are often incredibly difficult to read and understand. You will have to read them *at least* twice. Even very smart people have to struggle to grasp the insights, arguments, and explanations that philosophical texts contain.

7.1.3 Capacity for self-criticism

Philosophers are notoriously tough critics of intellectual work in general and written work in particular. This is all in the service of intellectual honesty. Be open to criticism and improvement. *You* should be the first person to discover and address the weaknesses in your arguments, explanations, and papers. But, when others point out flaws in your arguments, this is not a personal attack. Again, Mill's words are instructive:

> Human beings owe to each other help to distinguish the better from the worse, and encouragement to choose the former and avoid the latter. They should be forever stimulating each other to increased exercise of their higher faculties, and increased direction of their feelings and aims towards wise instead of foolish, elevating instead of degrading, objects and contemplations. ([1859] 1989: 76)

Incisive criticism can be as good as gold, because you are able to incorporate the insights of other smart people into the betterment of your own view. Of course, it is important that everyone – especially the critic – recognize that criticizing an argument and criticizing a person are very different enterprises.

7.1.4 Love of excellence

Philosophers take great pleasure in logical, literary, and scientific excellence. They hope their writings and lecturers will make a valuable contribution to the discussion of matters of fundamental human significance, as well as to the training of the next generation of participants in that discussion. In order to make such a contribution, you must be dedicated to producing clear, cogent, and well-supported arguments and faithful and informed interpretations of texts. Furthermore, some issues can only be addressed properly if you first study some science, art, foreign language, etc. Philosophers are among those intellectuals who find these challenges, these opportunities to expand and deepen their capabilities, to be exciting and, frankly, a great deal of fun.

7.2 Come to Class Prepared

Consider the alternatives: either you do not come to class or you come unprepared. In the first instance, you will be unable to benefit from the lectures of the instructor and the comments and discussion of your colleagues. You will also miss important announcements and instructions. The worst of it is, however, the fact that you have a responsibility to make a thoughtful contribution to the intellectual community of which you became a part by enrolling in your school. You have an important role to play in the cognitive and moral development of your colleagues and instructors and, if you do not participate, that obligation is left unfulfilled. In the second instance, if you come to class unprepared, then the lectures and discussions will not mean much to you. It is a significant advantage to have your questions answered in real-time, while you are working through the material. By asking questions in class, your ideas take center stage, as you invite the professor and the other students to mull over a problem with you. This can be highly-gratifying intellectually. It can also help you to improve your understanding of the texts in advance of writing a paper or taking an exam.

7.3 Ask Substantive Questions

Far too many of the questions students ask concern: (a) the expectations for papers; (b) the content of exams; (c) a grade they did not like; and (d) why philosophy is so hard. Students would do better to ask questions about the material they are covering in the course. It is a safe bet that if a student comes to a well-considered, well-researched understanding of the material, these other issues will take care of themselves.

7.4 Respect the Arduous Process of Careful Reading and Writing

Reading difficult texts will take a great deal of time. But it can give you a gratifying feeling of connection with other thoughtful and creative human beings. Additionally, it fosters an appreciation of the rich cultural heritage from which we may benefit if we pay attention. Similarly, writing philosophy papers is a slow, painstaking process. Philosophers expect everything you say in a paper to be crystal clear, rigorously argued, and well-documented by the philosophical texts you are discussing. You should only turn in for a grade a carefully-drafted paper. And other good writers should have critiqued previous drafts. This process is arduous but essential, because it is only by expressing your thoughts clearly that others will be able to discover and benefit from the insights you've had.

Philosophical writing functions not just to communicate arguments to other people, but also to develop the details of the insights we have had.[1] Often, we only realize how well or poorly we understand our own argument, let alone the arguments we are building on or criticizing, until we put pen to paper and work it through in a first draft. When I look back at my own first drafts, I am generally (a) amazed that I thought I was ready to write a draft when I understood things so incompletely, and then (b) impelled to further close reading and careful thinking, until I feel prepared to try again. Philosophers tend to believe that writing is an indispensable part of thinking through

---

[1] I am grateful to Coleen Zoller for urging me to discuss this aspect of philosophical writing.

difficult issues and arguments. And the arduous process of writing and rewriting, reading and rereading, is an essential aspect of your intellectual and scholarly development.

Students may not be aware that the materials they are working through in a philosophy course often overlap with the materials that their instructor is working through in her or his own philosophical research and writing. Two of the reasons for this practice should be noted. First, philosophers often feel that they do not really understand an argument unless they can explain it to someone else. Teaching is, in this respect, integral to the intellectual development of the instructor. Second, instructors in philosophy genuinely hope that their students will dig in to the materials, engage the issues and arguments, and share the fruits of their intellectual labors with the other students in class discussions and with the instructor in their papers. Students have the opportunity in their written work to make arguments, interpret passages, or raise issues that will make a real contribution to the progress of knowledge. If your instructor is teaching materials in his or her research area, then he or she will be well-positioned to steer your attention towards the current debates. And you will be, consequently, well-positioned to illuminate the issues and texts that are actively being debated.

7.5 Why is Philosophy So Hard to Do?

So much of what passes for culture today is fundamentally incompatible with patient, honest, careful, and rigorous thinking about the beliefs we rely upon to orient our lives. The things that pass for insight and analysis today – from the glib slogans of politicians to staged, televised "debates" – are diametrically opposed to focused, fair-minded consideration of what might actually be true (like it or not) and what justification (if any) we have for believing and behaving the way we do. If the most visible model of intellectual exchange – the political debate – consists of a disjointed public rehearsal of prefabricated sound bites, then it is likely that we have not been socially primed for a painstaking analysis of, for example, our concept of *personhood* and whether embryos are covered by that concept.

If philosophy is the activity of investigating concepts and justifying commitments, think of a *philosophical commitment* as a concept or justification that has been *adopted as adequate*.[2] That is to say, one undertakes a philosophical commitment whenever one accepts either that: (a) some concept under which one classifies an object captures the salient characteristics of the object; or (b) some reason provides adequate grounds for one rationally to believe some proposition. In this sense, everyone has philosophical commitments because everyone thinks that some of the concepts that they use to think about important issues are adequate and that some of the justifications they accept for important decisions are adequate too. The real question to ask when considering the value of doing philosophy is this: given that you will inevitably have philosophical commitments, would you rather they issue from your own insights and values or those of someone else?

Philosophers sometimes think they have done their best work when they have shown how the questions over which we tend to obsess might be ill-formed and how the answers to so-called "deep questions" might be more informed by preconceptions and misconceptions than penetrating insight. Philosophers take a special pleasure in restoring complexity to issues that have been oversimplified or made overly pedestrian by an insensitive and indifferent culture.

7.6 Why is Philosophy So Hard to Read?

Even after careful reading and study, there are times when you will still have no clue what the author is talking about. This happens to everyone. I feel this way when I read anything by G.W.F. Hegel.[3] If the text you are reading was translated, you might check for another translation to see how another translator handled a particularly vexing passage. Even better, if you read the original language, go read the author's own words. Two additional resources are available that should be consulted in this order. First, far too few students go to their teachers for help. Instructors take immense pleasure in working with

---

[2] This conception of philosophy is more fully elaborated in Chapter 8.

[3] Hegel (1770–1831) is one of the most important philosophers of the nineteenth century, known principally for his development of German Idealism. You may read his works if you take a course in Nineteenth-Century Philosophy, Contemporary Philosophy, Continental Philosophy, Ethics, Social & Political Philosophy or a seminar specifically on his philosophy.

students to find ways to make the texts accessible. Indeed, that was likely one of the reasons your instructor decided to teach philosophy for a living. Second, reading a commentator can sometimes be useful just to get your bearings. For example, it can be helpful to know ahead of time that certain terms have special meaning in the philosopher's vocabulary. And a commentator will probably alert you to those terms and their meaning. Of course, even if you find a commentator helpful, you still have to come to terms with the primary text in order to write your paper.[4]

Keep in mind that some of the most difficult-to-read philosophical texts are translations into English of texts that were already challenging in the original Greek, Latin, French, German, etc. And some of the most important philosophers we read literally had to invent the genre of philosophical writing in their respective languages. It is an amazing accomplishment to fashion for the first time in a given language a style and vocabulary for explicating our most fundamental beliefs. Students should try to understand the thoughts that stimulated the philosopher so intensely that he or she thought it was necessary to invent an idiom just to express them.

Most of the texts you will be assigned to read in philosophy courses were written by philosophers who are now dead. This presents at least two challenges to beginning students. First, philosophers of yore often employed a manner of expression that we moderns find unfamiliar and tedious. Second, although the problems they struggled with might be shared in common with you and your contemporaries – for example, whether it is always wrong to tell a lie – they will have inevitably: (a) directed their arguments at the sensibilities and preoccupations of *their* contemporaries (not yours); (b) situated their position in the context of the debates that were raging at *their* time (not yours); and (c) failed to benefit from hindsight and whatever advances were made since –

---

[4] See ℓ 44 and ℓ 45 for an explanation of what primary and secondary sources are and how to use them. Although there are reference books (which are discussed in ℓ 45) that may help you to understand what the philosopher meant by some term, a standard dictionary will almost never help. See especially ℓ 32 for more on why not. This is due to the fact that the important terms in a philosophical text are used *technically* (i.e., with specific meaning attached) and not in their everyday sense. See ℓ 42 for more on technical terminology.

and in some cases *made possible by* – their contribution to the discussion.

You have to understand the major players and positions with which the author was contending in order adequately to interpret a philosopher's text. However, just because you may have to understand the context does not mean that you have to talk about it. Philosophers study and often contribute to intellectual history. But what they aim to produce is usually something different. The point is that interesting philosophical argumentation often requires at least a nodding acquaintance with the intellectual milieu of the authors and problems you are addressing.[5]

7.7 On the Critical Nature of Philosophy and a Few Myths it is Useful to Discard

The point of explicating our concepts and studying our justifications is to subject our concepts and justifications to *critical scrutiny*. Some of our concepts will be inadequate to the phenomena to which they are supposed to apply. For example, perhaps the capabilities we normally associate with human personhood are not present in fetuses or embryos or blastocysts or zygotes; and, thus, the moral vocabulary we use to discuss abortion may be in need of reform. Some of the justifications we currently accept for our commitments (even our fundamental commitments) will, upon careful analysis, turn out to be inadequate. For example, perhaps the conduct of the criminal has nothing to do with the morality of capital punishment; and, thus, some arguments for the death penalty may be invalid. Philosophical reflection focuses on the adequacy of our concepts and justifications and tests them against what we know about the world and what we take to be good reasons for belief and action. One hopes that in doing philosophy we might be able to correct our views, hold fewer false beliefs, and make better, more rational choices.

---

[5] Oftentimes, commentators on philosophical texts will either discuss the pertinent intellectual history or point one to the historical literature that treats that context separately. In this case, as with all secondary sources, it is best to consult with your instructor before spending time in the secondary literature. Secondary sources in general are of uneven quality. Your instructor can direct you to reliable and reputable works.

7.7.1 The myth that everyone is
"entitled to their opinion"

Some people react defensively to critical scrutiny of their commitments, the justifications they make for undertaking them, and concepts they use to express them. I sometimes hear people say, "I am entitled to my own opinion." It is important to realize that this statement – like any other statement of fact – might be true and might be false. After all, being *entitled* to something means having a *legitimate* claim to something, having a *right* to it that others are obligated to respect.

Is it true as a matter of fact (or true by definition) that every belief I hold is legitimate just because I happen to hold it? Do I have adequate justification for every one of my important beliefs? Are other people bound to respect me as a rational and decent person no matter what I believe? The answer in each case is, plainly "No."

I have a constitutional right in the United States and maybe a human right to use my own intelligence to come to my own conclusions about the meaning of life and express those conclusions in a wide range of public actions. But in order to have standing in a community as a person who *knows*, reasons *validly*, believes *rationally*, and acts *rightly*, I have to throw my hat in the ring with everyone else and get to work giving reasons for what I think and do. Being entitled and justified are properties that a person acquires only by successfully providing rational support for his or her views. The bare fact that I happen to think something does not mean that I have been epistemically, logically, rationally or morally *successful*, any more than the fact that I happen to enter a race means that I have *won*.

I think people say "I am entitled to my own opinion" most often to indicate their desire to end a conversation. Perhaps they do not wish to have their opinion criticized any further by a particular person or in a particular way. Perhaps they are trying politely to end a conversation and extricate themselves from the company of a person with strange views or bad manners. These are each, at bottom, social defense mechanisms; and, used as such, they are perfectly reasonable. Only please let us not think that the statement "I am entitled to my own opinion" is literally true!

7.7.2 The myth that everyone's commitments are "true for them"

The expression "it is true for me" is, I think, an elliptical version of "it is true for me though it may be false for you." It is difficult to think of a good example of something that could be true for Ms. Awada but false for Mr. Baxter. The best example I can think of is an evaluative statement like "The world is a cold and unfriendly place." Ms. A might see things that way and Mr. B might not. The statement purports to make a claim about the world. So we must ask, "What would have to be the case *in the world* for a statement *about the world* (i.e., that it is a cold and unfriendly place) to be true?"

I suppose saying that the world is cold and unfriendly means something like *many of the objects in the world tend not to respond to friendly overtures with commensurate camaraderie.* There might be something to this, insofar as buildings and water and nitrogen atoms can be annoyingly indifferent to one's social charm. But, suppose that Mr. B disagreed, because he found comfort in nature's intelligent design, which (he was certain) was evidence of the love of the Creator for human beings. Now, Ms. A and Mr. B may respond to the facts with different emotions and associations. But neither has suggested that the facts confronted by Ms. A are any different from the facts confronted by Mr. B.

The person who thinks that "true for me" is a coherent concept may lodge the following objection. The attitudes that people take *towards objects* are among the facts that determine which sentences *about the object* are true. That is to say, some facts about objects are determined by the relations they bear to other objects. Thus, perhaps the property of the world at issue in our example is the relational property "*such-and-such* is perceived to be cold and unfriendly by *so-and-so.*" Since the world is perceived to be cold and unfriendly by Ms. A, the sentence "The world is perceived to be cold and unfriendly by Ms. A" is true; and since the world is not so perceived by Mr. B, the sentence "The world is perceived to be cold and unfriendly by Mr. B" is false. However, this does not show that what is true for Ms. A is false for Mr. B. Instead of *one* sentence that is true for Ms. A but false for Mr. B, we have *two* sentences: one is about Ms. A and true, while the other is about Mr. B and false.

Even if Mr. B disagrees with Ms. A about the character of the world, there is no reason they cannot agree as to how each of them individually perceives it.

Ms. A might say instead that Mr. B is applying the wrong criterion in his judgment. Perhaps considering the intricate, beautiful microstructure of the physical world is to look at the wrong *level* of the world in determining whether it is cold and unfriendly. She is talking about *objects* in the world, not the infinitesimal *constituents* of objects in the world. A parallel disagreement might occur if Ms. A and Mr. B were at an art gallery and Ms. A thought that a painting of a green square on a white canvas was a good painting, whereas Mr. B thought that it was either a very bad painting or a very good practical joke. Ms. A might say that the painting focuses the viewer's attention on *color itself* rather than on color as a means to differentiate space, which makes the painting interesting, which makes the painting good. Mr. B might say that the painting is neither beautiful nor technically superior, which makes the painting bad.

But are Ms. A and Mr. B really having a disagreement *about the painting*? Couldn't Mr. B grant Ms. A's point about the innovation of the painting in focusing on color? And couldn't Ms. A grant Mr. B's point about the painting not being beautiful or technically superior? Yet, couldn't they still disagree about whether the painting was *good*? Yes. And the reason they could is that they are disagreeing about what are the correct criteria to apply in making aesthetic judgments. But far from suggesting that Ms. A and Mr. B might each have their own private realm of aesthetic truth – such that what is true for one is false for the other – this disagreement is less about the qualities of the painting than about the nature of art. As these examples show, the initial impression that what is true for one person could be false for another *often* fades once we consider what people really mean when they make value judgments and what are the conditions under which these judgments are true.

Another context in which people raise the specter of statements that are "true for me" is in discussions of ethical judgments and religious belief. Culture A may view infanticide as morally justifiable whereas Culture B may view infanticide as a moral abomination. One might be tempted to say that it is true for Culture A that infanticide is morally right, whereas it is true for Culture B that infanticide is morally wrong. Here I think we have a proposal with some philosophical interest, if the suggestion is that all there is to the concept of truth is being accepted by a culture or an individual.

The suggestion could be put differently to focus on *being moral* rather than *being true*: all it means for an action to be morally right or wrong is for that action to be approved or disapproved according to some culture's standards of conduct. This view is called *moral relativism* – the view that there are no universally-valid moral principles, no moral facts that would make moral judgments objectively true or false – and it is an interesting philosophical position that is not at all silly, though it might still be wrong. But like any philosophical position worth taking, it is not *obviously* true (not even to relativists) that truth and morals are relative – far from it. Moral relativism has to overcome serious objections, such as the observation that cultures tend to be much less uniform and much more internally-contested than relativism lets on. So it is not really clear *to what* truth and morality could be relative if *cultures* are not monolithic and traditions speak with more than one voice (Appiah 1993: ch. 9; Bilgrami 1995; Nussbaum 2000: ch. 1).

For example, take any moral judgment that historians three-hundred years from now might attribute to twenty-first century citizens of the United States – for example, it was (or was not) morally justified for the United States to remove Sadam Hussein from power in Iraq – and ask yourself: (a) whether every US citizen today agrees with this moral judgment; and (b) whether there is something called "American principles of right and justice" that would unambiguously and uncontroversially – that is, without any significant evidence pointing the other direction – issue such a moral judgment. The obvious answer to both questions is "No," which indicates that a culture's values and traditions tend to be much more fluid and contested than some relativists assume. The upshot of all this is that relativism – like any other philosophical position – has to be clearly articulated and rigorously defended.

As with the expression "everyone is entitled to their opinion," I think that most of the time when people say "well, it's true for me," they are not really asserting a proposition they take to be true, but are rather utilizing another social coping mechanism. Again, people sometimes wish to end a conversation for whatever reason. And even philosophers understand the need to do that from time to time! Nonetheless, if you actually want to make the very controversial philosophical claim that truth or morality is relative, do not assert it with the same casual indifference as blowing your nose.

Some of the time, people are expressing the laudable and humane sentiment that the views of other people, cultures, and eras ought not to be dismissed or ridiculed because they happen to come to different conclusions on important issues than we do. The views of other people are at least as worthy of being understood and examined as are our own. This is part of what it means to participate in the "conversation of mankind" (to use Michael Oakeshott's[6] expression).

Far too often, we encounter people who display impatience, intolerance, and ignorance with respect to views that differ from their own. Some people (quite mistakenly) respond to such displays of bad intellectual form by denying that cross-cultural and interpersonal criticisms are legitimate, asserting that each culture and perspective has its own rightful claim on morality and truth. As usual, however, the right way to respond to an unenlightened interlocutor is to address the source of the error – to point out the impatience, intolerance, and ignorance. There is no need to jump precipitously into the rough waters of the relativism/universalism debate if your only aim is to restore civility and fair-mindedness to a discussion.

---

[6] Michael Oakeshott (1901–90) was a political philosopher who taught at the London School of Economics.

8

What Does it Mean to *Do* Philosophy?

I should emphasize at the outset that the view I explore in this chapter is *one* view of philosophy. I offer it only to orient the reader to *some* of the main concerns of contemporary philosophers, in hopes of giving the reader a better idea of what he or she will likely encounter in reading philosophical texts and what his or her instructors likely expect to encounter in philosophy papers.

Philosophers do not often agree on what philosophy is or what counts as philosophical thinking and writing. Philosophy is distinctive in that asking "What is philosophy, how should it be done, and why is it important?" is an enduring component of philosophical inquiry, not a symptom of epistemic or methodological crisis, as might be suspected when another branch of inquiry reexamines its identity. Doubtless, your instructors and the texts you study will present alternative views of philosophy that deserve careful study. Nonetheless, my hope is that what follows will help to prepare you to wrestle with those alternatives and develop your own view of what philosophy is and how it ought to be done.

Answering questions about who we are and how we fit into the rest of the world is the first stage in the process of making reasoned practical decisions about how we will live our lives. You will probably think differently about the point of your life and your obligations to others depending on whether you think of yourself as a product of natural selection, a fallen being created in the image of God or a purposeless being in a meaningless world. We all probably acquire a view of the human condition just in virtue of being exposed to the views of our families, teachers, religions, and cultures. But one of the requirements of intellectual maturity is playing an active, critical, and reflective role in fashioning one's self-understanding.

One way to start thinking about the value of philosophy is to ask the following questions: Who stands to gain if the majority of people have not carefully thought through issues of fundamental moral, political, and scientific importance? What sort of moral or political act is it to think carefully and creatively about the justifications that are offered for economic, scientific, political, and social policies? What would a society be like if citizens saw philosophical inquiry as one of their civic duties?

There is an assumption that is shared by Enlightenment thinkers and some of their most strident critics "that social freedom is inseparable from enlightened thought" (Horkheimer and Adorno [1944] 1995: xiii).[1] Philosophy is an activity in which issues that matter dearly to us are thought through clearly and carefully. Commitments and concepts are subjected to vigorous public scrutiny. By explaining and justifying ourselves to each other under conditions of free and open inquiry, we get closer to each other, and hopefully to the truth.

8.1 Philosophers Inquire into Our Concepts and Commitments

Philosophers like to take harmless-sounding propositions that people usually are happy to state and accept without a second thought and show how, if such propositions are true, strange and unacceptable consequences logically follow. We are commonly quite happy to say that everything that happens is *determined* to happen by antecedent causes; but, what then becomes of our ability *freely* to make decisions about our lives? We do not think twice about saying that a person's character is *determined* by her or his upbringing and environment; but, then how can we ever hold a person morally

---

[1]   Consider also Michel Foucault's position regarding critical reflection on the historical formation of subjectivity, which he takes to be the philosophical *ethos* of Enlightenment: "I continue to think that this task requires work on our limits, that is, a patient labor giving form to our impatience for liberty" (1998: 319).

accountable for her or his actions? We may contend that truth is *relative* to a historical epoch, a culture or even a person; but, then what becomes of the distinction between *what is true* and what some person (or discipline or culture or epoch) happens to think at a given time?

The commitments that generate these conundrums might initially sound quite reasonable. For example, isn't the notion that all events have determining causes one of the most basic principles of natural science? Nonetheless, the *consequences* of even the most ordinary-sounding statement can be deeply troubling. After all, it is part of our self-conception that at least sometimes we can choose *freely*, even if most events are causally determined, that people can be held morally *accountable* for their actions in a way that clocks cannot, and that at least some propositions – *that Mt Everest is taller than the Empire State Building*, for example – are universally *true*. Once we realize the difficulties in which we become entangled if we accept even reasonable-sounding propositions, we take a more cautious attitude towards our assumptions and intuitions.

Notice that, considered by itself, the suggestion that each culture has its own truths is not particularly troubling. It only *becomes* troubling when we consider: (a) how this suggestion fits with other statements we accept; and (b) what the world would have to be like for this statement to be true. Is it coherent to think that "Mt Everest is taller than the Empire State Building" is true for everyone everywhere *and* that there is no universal truth? What would the world have to be like in order for "Mt Everest is taller than the Empire State Building" to be *true* in some places but *false* in others? By asking questions like these, philosophers try to put propositions in their logical context by showing how they follow from, support, contradict or are irrelevant to certain other propositions. In this way, propositions are presented as logically interrelated.

In our everyday lives, we do not usually pay specific attention to the interrelations among propositions. And, for this reason, the structure of these interrelations remains implicit. Philosophers have used the metaphors of a *web* or a *network* to illustrate the way that beliefs or propositions are interconnected (e.g., Quine and Ullian 1978). Philosophy might be viewed as an activity that aims to make these interconnections *explicit* so that we may understand and evaluate

them. For example, Robert Brandom[2] has argued that one of the
central tasks of philosophers is "the development and application of
expressive tools with which to make explicit what is implicit in the use
of concepts" (Brandom 2004: 74).

I think Brandom has this exactly right, so I would like to try to
explain in what follows what I understand by *making concepts and
commitments explicit*. Basically, doing philosophy means studying the
structure of our theoretical and practical commitments as they are
articulated through concept use. That is to say, by doing philosophy
we find ways to increase our awareness of what it takes to make a
statement true, what counts as a reason to accept a statement, what
counts as a good inference from a statement, and what sorts of theoretical and practical commitments a person undertakes in making a
statement.

8.2 Philosophy Explicates What is Implicit in Our Concepts and Commitments

We express a commitment whenever we assert a sentence that we take
to be true. If I say, "Stem cell research is morally wrong," I am saying
that a concept (*morally wrong*) applies to a certain thing (*stem cell
research*). This moral judgment expresses a commitment for which I
can be held accountable as a rational person making a truth claim.
Other rational persons will deem me to be entitled to assert this moral
judgment – that is, they will consider me a truth-holder as regards this
application of a moral concept – depending on whether I am able to
offer adequate reasons for my assertion.

One way of revealing what it *means* to say "Stem cell research is
morally wrong" is to ask what would qualify as a *reason* for saying that
something is morally wrong. Uncertainty about what is a genuine
moral reason points up uncertainty about what the moral judgment
means in the first place. For example, although the assertion "Stem
cell research is morally wrong" seems commonplace, ask yourself

---

[2] Brandom teaches at the University of Pittsburgh and is active in a field called
"semantics" which includes the theory of meaning, the theory of truth, and the theory
of logical relations. A list of his publications can be found at <http://www.pitt.
edu/~rbrandom/>.

whether it is patently clear: (a) what facts would tend to show that "Stem cell research is morally wrong" is true; and (b) what the consequences would be for how we think and act if that statement is true. If the answer to the first question is "moral facts," then we require an explanation of what those are, how they differ from other sorts of facts (if they do), and how we discover them. Moreover, if the answer to the first question is "facts about the emotions of the person asserting the sentence regarding stem cell research," a view in metaethics called "emotivism," then question (b) looms large, as we have to ask whether one person's negative emotions have any bearing upon science policy or, indeed, on the moral judgments of anyone else. Thinking philosophically about the morality of stem cell research requires us to analyze the concepts we use to make moral judgments and the justifications that entitle us to take moral judgments to be true.

By "concept use," I simply mean forming a thought or proposition (for example, *that snow is white*). We use concepts to attribute properties to objects. It is an interesting question whether concepts are abstract objects in our minds, or patterns of neurons in our brains, or whether having a concept is nothing other than knowing how to use a word. I would like to remain agnostic in the ensuing discussion as to which among these (or other) alternatives is preferable, and simply focus on the use of concepts to think thoughts and form propositions that might be true of the world.

Imagine that you and I are watching a pot of water on a stovetop, waiting for it to boil, at which point we will call out "Boiling!" Imagine that there is a thermometer suspended in the water that plays a recorded voice saying "Boiling!" when it registers 212°F. When the water reaches the magic temperature, imagine that you, I, and the thermometer each report "Boiling!" in unison. What is the difference between what we have done and what the thermometer has done?[3]

The view of philosophy I am exploring here holds that whereas *we* have applied a concept and undertaken a commitment to the truth of a statement – that is, we have applied the concept "boiling" to the stuff in the pan called "water" – *the thermometer's noise* is a mechanical

---

[3] Here, I follow the tenor of Brandom's discussion of concept use in his (2001: 17ff).

effect of a change in the water's temperature. When we use a concept, we undertake a commitment that can be supported by giving reasons for our application of the concept to the phenomena. Presumably, you and I reported "boiling" *because* we saw bubbles bubbling or steam steaming or whatever. We could cite these observations as reasons for applying the concept "boiling" to the water. And, in the absence of these or similar observations (and the facts that prompted these observations), our use of the concept "boiling" to make a claim about the water would likely be challenged by our peers. If our statement is unsupported by relevant observations, we run the risk of breaking the rules according to which the concept "boiling" is applied to stuff like water.

When I assert *that* something is the case, this is a particular form of public action whereby I recommend that we take a statement to be true. By asserting *that the water is boiling* I take a position that brings with it certain responsibilities. For example, I should be prepared to state my reasons for making this assertion. And my grasp of the concepts – indeed, my rationality – will be judged according to whether the other assertions I make and actions I undertake are consistent with this statement and the justification I bring to support it. If I perform successfully in the game of giving and asking for reasons, I may acquire the social status as someone who *knows*, someone who *is justified in believing* or someone who *has a concept*. Alternatively, when the thermometer accurately reports that the water is boiling, we do not say that it is justified in believing that the water is boiling or that it applied the concept *boiling* to the liquid in which it is immersed. We simply say that it *works* in the manner of a useful tool.

If you and I apply the concept "boiling" to the water, we undertake a commitment that can itself serve as a reason for other commitments. For example, we might state that another person who just came into the kitchen and picked up the pot ought to take care not to be burned. If we did not make the connection between boiling water and being burned, it would be open to question whether we had really grasped the conceptual content of "boiling" and whether our statement was completely rational after all. It is because using a concept to make a claim has a concrete impact on what we *do* (including what we *think*) that concept use is part of the social practice of using language to organize our behavior and express ourselves.

Consider, for example, the concept of knowledge. What does it mean to say of some person (call her "S") that she *knows* some proposition (call it "p")? Consider how we might try to answer this question just by focusing on the concept itself. We might think about how a child uses the concept or the word "know." If a five year-old child is asked by a new acquaintance how old she is, and the child responds "I don't know," her mother might encourage her by saying "Sure you do – how many candles were on your birthday cake?" If the child is able to remember how many candles were on her birthday cake, and is aware that the birthday girl gets one candle on her cake for every year she has lived, would it be correct to attribute to the child knowledge of her own age? Must the thought "I am five years old" occur explicitly to the girl in order for it to be the case that she *knows* her age? More generally, can a person *know* something of which she is (presently) unaware?

By considering this example we have begun to experiment with a word or concept by considering whether it would be correct to attribute knowledge to a particular person given what she says, how she behaves, what she is aware of, what she believes, etc. And since it is a hypothetical example, we can fiddle with the facts of our story to test whether changing certain conditions while holding others constant would change our intuitions about whether the concept is appropriately applied in the new case. For example, we could consider the case where the girl parrots back "I'm five" whenever she is asked her age, but is unable to apply the concept "five" to the fingers on one hand and cannot explain what it means for her to *be* five. Does she know her age under these circumstances?

This manner of approaching the problem is called a *thought experiment*. We use thought experiments to help make explicit what is implicit in our use of concepts. By exploring the contours of a concept – testing the limits of its appropriate application to specific cases – we become better acquainted with the terms we use to describe the world. This process of exploration may cause us to see that we have been using a concept that was inadequate to the phenomenon it was supposed to capture, that the *thing* as we encounter it is more (or less) complex than the *concept* we use when we think and talk about it.

Another one of the expressive resources for making explicit what is implicit in our use of concepts is *logical inquiry*. There are two primary modes of logical inquiry. First, logical *analysis* breaks down complex propositions into their simpler constituent parts. Logical analysis shows that, for example, if I believe the complex proposition *that the present king of France is bald*, I have implicit commitments to the simpler propositions *that someone is now the king of France* and *that this person is bald* (Russell 1905). Second, logical *synthesis* (a.k.a. "inference") tells us what *else* we are on the hook for if we hold a certain set of beliefs. Logical synthesis shows that, for example, if I believe *that all humans are mortal* and *that Socrates is a human* then I am implicitly committed to the proposition *that Socrates is mortal*. It is through logical inquiry that we make the full range of our commitments explicit by inquiring into what is logically implicit in them. The logical constituents and logical consequences of our commitments may never have occurred to us; and, thus, we may not accept them, now or ever. But logical inquiry shows us what we *ought* to accept given the statements we *do* accept.[4]

I have explained (following Brandom) why philosophical scrutiny of concepts and the justifications we give for their application is essentially an exercise in explication, making explicit what is implicit. This is one plausible view of what it means to do philosophy. So, with the basics well in hand, let us consider a few more examples to become better acquainted with this conception of philosophical explication.

Suppose I said that stem cell research is morally wrong at a medical conference in a room full of doctors and nurses. I might have to field a question from the audience asking how I differentiate morally permissible scientific experiments from morally prohibited ones. As I begin to mention those factors that informed my conclusion, I will be *making explicit what I mean* by saying that stem cell research is morally wrong. If I say that the costs outweigh the benefits, the audience would know that by *immoral* I mean *inefficient*. If I

---

[4] The Scottish philosopher David Hume (1711–76) pointed out that one cannot derive a normative conclusion from factual premises. That is to say, one cannot derive an "ought" from an "is" ([1740] 2000: Book III, ch. 1, sec. 1, par. 28). It might appear that I have made this mistake in the text above, but that is wrong. The conclusion is elliptical, and would be completed ". . . on pain of irrationality." The desire to be deemed rational or the fact that one would have violated a norm of rationality supplies the normative premise to validly derive the conclusion.

say that stem cell research violates the sanctity of human life, the audience would know that by *immoral* I mean *desecrating*. If I say that stem cell research violates the norm of medical ethics requiring informed consent from all participants in scientific and medical experiments, the audience would know that by *immoral* I mean *negligent* or otherwise *illegal*, e.g., under the Nuremberg Code [1947] (1949).

If someone responds that efficiency is not a moral consideration, then she would be challenging the *adequacy* of the concept I used to the phenomenon in question (namely, moral wrong). She would be saying that economic efficiency-talk does not get at the morally salient aspects of stem cell research. If someone suggested that desecration just is not a persuasive consideration for setting public policy in a society where people construe sacredness differently, she would be challenging the *significance* of the concept I applied in the context in which I applied it.

Alternatively, if I say that stem cell research is morally wrong, I am presumably saying something that might be true or might be false.[5] How are we able to tell the difference between a true moral claim and a false one? Is a true moral claim like a true scientific claim in the sense that there are empirical facts that make it true? Is a true moral claim like a true claim in mathematics in that we can expect a formal proof? Or if *truth* is too difficult a concept to apply to moral claims, then what about *justification*? What considerations could one adduce to begin to *justify* a moral judgment?

We will begin to reflect *philosophically* when we begin to wonder about: (a) the significance and adequacy of the concepts we use; and (b) the justifications that can be supplied for using those concepts to

---

[5] For ease of exposition, I want to assume that statements about moral right/wrong are statements that can be true or false. This view is called "cognitivism" in moral theory. *Non*cognitivist theories of ethics hold that moral statements do not aim to state facts; that is, instead of functioning to make truth claims, they express emotions or preferences or prescribe behavior to oneself or others. Since cognitivism and noncognitivism are not views about the morality of actions, but rather are views about what is at stake when we theorize about the morality of actions, they belong to the field, not of ethics, but of *meta*ethics (that is, the study of ethics). Nonetheless, students are likely to encounter these ideas in an Ethics course.

make truth claims. In the example we are considering, philosophical reflection would focus on the concept of moral wrong and the justifications that could be offered for applying that concept to stem cell research.

The issues raised in the last two paragraphs show a few examples of what philosophers *do* when they begin to *think philosophically*. Yet, the statement we were considering was abstract. So, let us consider a more concrete example from the current political debates in the United States. When President George W. Bush announced his administration's position on stem cell research, he reported confronting the question whether frozen embryos – the most promising source for stem cell lines at the time – are *human life* (Bush 2001). Usually, we have no difficulty applying the concept "human life" to (or withholding it from) the beings we encounter in our everyday lives. Can you ever recall having been mistaken in taking something for a *human* being that you learned later was some *other* sort of being? But embryos (especially frozen embryos) are a problematic case where reasonable and well-informed people have vigorously disagreed as to whether they should be considered examples of human life.

Well – what *does* it mean to apply the concept "human life" to a bunch of cells, including you and me? One of the reasons it is difficult to know whether something is *human life* is that we mean a lot more by calling an organism a *human* being than a mere biological classification. Even cadavers are members of the species and share the same genome as the rest of us. But the statement that a cadaver is human life would be false by definition. If we use the classification *living homo sapiens*, we have to say what processes are associated with *living* as opposed to dead *homo sapiens*. Once we come up with a checklist – locomotion, respiration, nutrition, cellular (re)generation, and whatever else – we will inevitably encounter examples of organisms that exhibit some but not all of the processes; and there will still be a question as to which processes any *human* life must exhibit. Or is "human life" rather expressing a thicker concept, referring instead to specifically human characteristics and capabilities that qualify a member of the species *homo sapiens* as a human *person*? For example, perhaps any human being that deserves the title "human life" ought to be capable of cognition and conscious feeling. In this case, some fetuses might count, but some brain dead people and anencephalics (those born without brains) might not.[6] There is clearly much to wrestle with in the notion that a frozen embryo is *human life*.

Despite these difficulties, we have managed to make some progress just by reflecting a little about the classification. One of the reasons we call something *human life* is its genetic make-up. Another reason is that it exhibits or is capable of certain characteristic biological processes. These factors may not decide the issue, but they are *reasons* for saying that an organism is a human life. And one of the ways we can investigate the content of our concepts is by asking what would count as reasons for attributing the concept to something.[7]

Another way we investigate the content of our concepts is by asking, "What *other* propositions would one have to defend if one believed that an embryo is human life?" Attending to what necessarily follows if a proposition is true is part of *logical inquiry*. Logic helps us to make our rational obligations explicit by looking at the implicit consequences of our commitments. For example, suppose I hold the following beliefs:

---

[6]   One of the most publicized events of 2005 in the United States raised these issues vividly. The Florida Second District Court of Appeal found that Theresa Marie Schiavo lacked the capacity for cognitive function (given that most if not all of her cerebral cortex had deteriorated and was replaced by cerebral spinal fluid), and that, since she had earlier expressed a desire that her life not be artificially prolonged in such a state, the court would permit Michael Schiavo, her husband and legal guardian, to remove her nutrition and hydration tube (*In re Guardianship of Schiavo* 2001). However, *no one* in the surrounding legal battle ever suggested that the concept "human life" did not apply to Ms. Schiavo. She was not brain dead, as her brain stem continued to function, permitting, for example, respiration and digestion. Rather, she was in a permanent vegetative state. So what is it about brain stem activity that convinced all the parties that she evidenced *human life*? Must human life evidence brain stem activity? Or is brain stem activity just one characteristic among others that qualify a being as human life? Are our moral obligations to respect and protect Ms. Schiavo's life and dignity different depending on which characteristics are present? Ms. Schiavo died on March 31, 2005. The public discussion – which was, on the whole, appallingly facile, question-begging, politicized, and self-serving – illustrates one result of ideologically asserting commitments, rather than philosophically explicating them.
[7]   Incidentally, concepts evolve (as they inevitably do) when new characteristics are accepted as reasons for concept use and new consequences are accepted as following from concept use (Brandom 2001, especially ch. 1).

1   Any being that lacks the capacity for human consciousness is not
    a human life.
2   Human consciousness is impossible without a human brain.
3   One-celled human zygotes do not have human brains.

It follows logically from (1)–(3) that:

4   One-celled human zygotes are not human lives.

This consequence of my beliefs may not have occurred to me explicitly.
However, inquiring into what else *must be true* if my current beliefs
are true points up further commitments that are implicit in my
acknowledged commitments. I have a rational obligation to either:

☑   face the music and accept the consequences of my commitments
    (like it or not); *or*
☑   revise my original commitments that led me to the conclusion.

If I reject the conclusion as false, then I must not grasp the content
of my beliefs, or else I am unable to appreciate the consequences of
my beliefs. Either way, I will not be taken as a person who is *justified*
in undertaking my commitments, because I do not appear even to
understand them.

   Whether we are trying to understand the full import of a statement
in isolation (the bald king of France example) or in conjunction with
other statements (the zygote example), the purpose of doing philosophy is to lay out in plain view our concepts, our commitments, and
our reasons so that we can assess their adequacy and their underlying
values.

8.3 Philosophical Reflection and the Public Use of Reason

Philosophical reflection involves asking after the reasons for the commitments and actions that shape our lives. We want to understand the
reasons why, for example, it is immoral to execute a murderer (if it is)
or why human cloning is incompatible with human dignity (if it is).
If we want an explanation for why we ought not to execute murderers

or why we ought not to pursue human cloning, then we need arguments – the chains of reasons that tell us why we come down where we do on these issues.

However, philosophers develop explanations dialogically. Philosophers engage others in the search for reasons by communicating their insights and challenging others with critique, argument, and bold theorizing. Philosophers communicate their thoughts and questions to others in large part because they believe: (a) that they have a moral obligation to help cultivate the human potential for rational thought *by engaging it*; and, (b) that the human potential for rational thought is best (and maybe only) cultivated *in dialogue* with others.

Nevertheless, some philosophers do not address themselves in the first instance to identifiable interlocutors. Sometimes philosophical investigations are more personal and introspective than social and inter-subjective. Still, even these reflections involve a use of reason that engages others. First, philosophical reflection is often prompted by the insights and arguments of other people. Thus, we are engaged with others as we work to understand the reasoning supporting their views. Second, even an author such as Friedrich Nietzsche[8] – who could write, in a sardonically-titled chapter "Why I Write Such Good Books," "that today one doesn't hear me and doesn't accept my ideas is not only understandable, it even seems right to me" – still contemplates a reader for whom reading his works "would raise one to a higher level of existence than 'modern' man could attain" (Nietzsche [1888] 1967: 259). So, philosophers who cannot find their intended audience still direct their arguments to an audience that is, it is hoped, on the way.

Whatever illumination we might gain individually by the light of reason, philosophers feel a duty and desire to inquire into things further, to set out the rational grounds of an insight and delve into its logical and practical consequences, to compare the results of their use of reason with the results of those who have reasoned things through in the past. In short, whatever the outcome of isolated

---

[8]   Nietzsche (1844–1900) held a Chair of Classical Philology at the University of Basel for about a decade. He developed trenchant criticisms of traditional philosophical views of truth, knowledge, aesthetics, and, especially, Judeo-Christian morality. He is often associated with Existentialism and famously wrote: "God is dead. God remains dead. And we have killed him. How shall we comfort ourselves, the murderers of all murderers?" ([1882] 1974: 181–2).

speculation and analysis, philosophers feel compelled to return to the community of rational persons and present their discoveries as rational achievements, as truths for which reasons can be given, and which can stand as reasons warranting belief in other, yet unrecognized truths. This point may be put in a normative key: philosophers are generally interested in articulating conceptions and justifications that *deserve to be* respected, acknowledged and, perhaps, accepted by other rational beings.

Philosophy as an activity – as something people do to deepen their awareness of the rational grounds of their beliefs and the contours of their concepts – is importantly different from modes of thought in which institutions, texts, and experiences are authoritative. Indeed, it is the very nature of authority to preempt one's own independent exercise of reason (see, e.g., Raz 1994: 198). Conversely, philosophy is a manner of reflection in which a person is right to form and hold a belief only if it is the result of rational conviction, which is generally achieved through argument based on publicly-available evidence.

The difference between philosophy and other modes of understanding becomes readily apparent if we canvass the various modes of addressing the morality of stem cell research, some of which are philosophical and some of which are decidedly not. Among the possible approaches to a tough moral question, we could:

- ☑ ask God;
- ☑ ask our religious leaders;
- ☑ take a vote;
- ☑ ask the experts;
- ☑ run a cost–benefit analysis and see which policies produce the greatest good for the greatest number of people;
- ☑ ask which courses of action are coherent with our self-understanding as human beings (e.g., as rational, autonomous, enlightened, or fallen beings); or
- ☑ think through what "human life" means in biology and our other traditions that take a view on human life, and ask whether these conceptions are coherent and adequate to the phenomena they aim to capture.

These are all modes of addressing difficult issues that enjoy their own spheres of legitimacy, and we rely on these modes all the time.

Nevertheless, philosophers tend to be primarily concerned with two activities: clarifying our concepts and testing the justifications of our beliefs. So it is the last mode that would be the best candidate for a philosophical inquiry (though the penultimate mode is a decent candidate too).

There are several areas of philosophy that might take an interest in the question whether we should pursue stem cell research. Philosophers interested in ethics might take it as a question about whether we have duties to undifferentiated masses of cells or what the moral impact would be of technological intervention into the biological development of human beings. Philosophers of science might think about how political decisions shape scientific research programs and what constitutes "legitimate" scientific inquiry. Political philosophers might ask how scarce intellectual and fiscal resources ought to be allocated in promoting certain research programs over others.

It is helpful in thinking about the aims of philosophy to keep in mind that we have an enormously difficult time making collaborative decisions on socially and politically important matters. It is difficult to convince your peers to adopt your conception of human life if they do not share your religious or scientific perspective (witness, for example, the contemporary impasses over abortion and euthanasia). The fact that others do not share your conceptions does not, of course, prevent you from scrutinizing their deepest premises, nor does it prevent them from scrutinizing yours. But if the grounds of one's convictions are irrevocable commitments to authority or inscrutable experiences of God's will, what room is there for conceptual and logical inquiry to move us towards policies and decisions that are responsive to reasons that any human being can credit? In other words, how must we approach thorny questions of fundamental human significance (and the decisions that inevitably follow) so that our human capacity for rationality plays a constitutive role in how we think and act?

Understanding the justifications for our basic commitments is not so perplexing in every domain as it is where philosophers tend to concentrate (i.e., the good, the true, and the beautiful). Statements are frequently made whose justifications are well within the grasp of anyone willing to take up the inquiry. If I ask a physicist, who has just reported the result of some measurement, how I know that she did not just make up the answer, she may well reply: "I don't care if you believe me or not! If you are such a skeptical person, why don't you carry out the measurement yourself?" That is to say, part of what keeps empirical inquiry honest (and thus highly respected in our culture) is the availability of *intersubjective confirmation*: other people can participate in the inquiry, check our work, and improve upon it if necessary. It is much less clear how intersubjective testing and confirmation might apply to premises derived from personal revelation or authoritative traditions or texts.[9]

Like science, one of the central goals of philosophy is to use evidence and argument to facilitate intersubjective inquiry – searching for insight by investigating reasons in dialogue with others. That is to say, philosophy is the sort of activity that aims to transcend the merely subjective realm of private experience and personal conviction by studying essentially social phenomena (concepts and justifications) by using essentially public tools (rational arguments, explanations, and criticisms addressed to a community of inquirers). With only an imperfect grasp of truth, we humans are constantly in the predicament of having to make tough choices under conditions of uncertainty. Philosophers tend to think that (a) greater clarity about the concepts we use to think about ourselves and the world, and (b) a deeper understanding of the reasons we have to think as we do, will help us come to commitments and decisions that *even if wrong* are commitments and decisions that made good use of our capacity to discern the truth.

The unexamined life just does not appear worthwhile to us (as Plato famously wrote in the *Apology* [1997(c): 38a]), the sorts of beings who think of themselves as intellectually acute and emotionally attuned. This is not to say that one's life can somehow be justified by examining it or that examination will necessarily point up certain eternal truths. Rather, by examining our lives, testing our self-conceptions, evaluating our practical and theoretical reasoning, we aim to infuse

---

[9] Yet everybody has to defer to authority and tradition, at least some of the time. No one bothers to verify the atomic weights of elements in chemistry class, for example. And none of us is irrational for "blindly" trusting the periodic table in that case. So how do we distinguish those cases when reliance upon authority is rational and those when it is not? I would suggest that the possibility for independent confirmation has *something* to do with the distinction. Students should take an epistemology or philosophy of science class to pursue this issue further.

our commitments and actions with the best of which we are capable. The desired result is that we will be able to act with that degree of autonomy that human beings demand for themselves and esteem in others.

Philosophers offer competing conceptions of autonomy. According to one account, it was characteristic of the modern era that people would accept authority only if it respected individual autonomy. Consequently, people were drawn towards self-determination in politics and ethical principles rooted in the good of rational agents. Jürgen Habermas[10] described this drive towards autonomy by stating that modernity "has to create its normativity out of itself" (Habermas 1990: 7). An autonomous agent, on this view, is subject to the law that derives from its own rational nature. It is self-legislating (*auto + nomos*). Alternatively, a will subject to a normative authority other than its own rational nature is heteronomous, since norms are given by some other measure than our rational nature (Kant [1785] 1964: 108–9; [1788] (1993): 33). Whatever we make of this Kantian approach to the legitimacy of norms, it is at least true to say that autonomous agents are those that deliberate for themselves and take responsibility for the fruits of their deliberations. Both of these acts require an agent to assess the merits of the alternatives. The exercise of judgment and self-reflection in this manner "are distinctively human capabilities, the exercise of which contribute in an essential way to human flourishing" (Shapiro 2002: 388), all the more so when exercised in dialogue with others.

It may seem incongruous that I am emphasizing the public nature of philosophical inquiry when, practically speaking, doing philosophy involves vastly more time spent alone in solitary reflection and patient reading and writing (and then re-reading and re-writing) than it does in pubic deliberation. For example, while Descartes identifies logical deduction as one source of knowledge, he takes its results to be uncertain to the extent that its constituent premises are not clearly and

---

[10] Habermas is Emeritus Professor in the Institute for Philosophy at the Johann Wolfgang Goethe Universität at Frankfurt am Main, Germany and Permanent Visiting Professor in the Department of Philosophy at Northwestern University. He is associated with the Frankfurt School of Critical Theory and has written widely on social theory, political liberalism, and the theory of communication.

distinctly perceived by the intellectual faculty, the light of reason ([1644] (1985): 290). The faculty of knowledge must grasp the indubitable truth of the elements of the deduction in order for the argument to yield certainty. Thus, on Descartes' account, rational argument has an important role to play in gaining knowledge. But it is neither necessary nor sufficient to grasp the most fundamental truths. It is not apparent why, as I have been arguing, the *public* use of reason might on this model be integral to rational insight.

Consider another counterexample to the view that philosophy involves the public use of reason. Aristotle held that philosophy is knowledge of the truth – that is to say, theoretical knowledge of first principles and causes, which constitutes wisdom (1984(b): II.993b20–21 and I.982a4–5). An individual comes to theoretical knowledge by surveying and internalizing, through contemplation, the eternal blueprints of being (1984(a): III.430a3–5).[11] Further, an individual does not need interlocutors in order to contemplate the truth: "the wise man, even when by himself, can contemplate the truth, and the better the wiser he is; he can perhaps do so better if he has fellow-workers, but still he is the most self-sufficient" (1984(c): X.1177a32–34). Considering Aristotle's conception of philosophy, which is similar to Descartes' insofar as truths may be grasped directly through intuition, points up the need for me to make a distinction that will clarify the view of philosophy I am articulating.

I am not arguing that in order to know the truth, gain theoretical knowledge, or delve into deep existential questions we need to engage in the public use of reason. Contemplation is not the same as argument or explication, especially insofar as the latter activities may be directed towards facilitating rational consensus in the face of manifest dissonance on moral and political issues. I am also not arguing against forms of metaphysical speculation that may bring clarity to the most basic questions of human existence. In fact, this understanding of philosophy has recently been reinvigorated by someone who set forth a sustained reflection upon the relationship between philosophy and religious faith (with which metaphysical speculation is sometimes conflated) and who vigorously defended the autonomy of philosophical

---

[11] This colloquialism is meant to capture Aristotle's term *ta noeta*, that is, actual noetic forms.

inquiry, Pope John Paul II[12]: "Driven by the desire to discover the ultimate truth of existence, human beings seek to acquire those universal elements of knowledge which enable them to understand themselves better and to advance in their own self-realization" (1998: §4). This conception of philosophy is oriented around fundamental metaphysical questions, such as "the meaning and ultimate foundation of human, personal and social existence" (1998: §5). Yet the insights of reason and philosophy are not mystically revealed. They convince us, in part, because they may be intersubjectively corroborated and they are tested by rigorous argumentation (1998: §§4, 29). So, regardless of whether we may grasp truth on our own, philosophy is a form of investigation where we reason things out together.

In a quite similar vein, Robert Nozick[13] noted that "[t]he word philosophy means the love of wisdom" (1993: xi). Nonetheless, he explained:

> what philosophers really love is reasoning. They formulate theories and marshal reasons to support them, they consider objections and try to meet these, they construct arguments against other views. Even philosophers who proclaim the limitations of reason – the Greek skeptics, David Hume, doubters of the objectivity of science – all adduce reasons for their views and present difficulties for opposing ones. Proclamations or aphorisms are not considered philosophy unless they also enshrine and delineate reasoning (*ibid*).

On the view I am urging, whatever other vocation reason may have, the role of reason *in philosophy* is not to intuit ultimate truths or come into mystical acquaintance with Being, but rather to develop and test the rational grounds of our commitments in dialogue with others.

But why should we think that "our rationality expresses itself not only in our deliberation and reasoning, nor in any other specific act

---

[12] Before becoming Pope John Paul II, Karol Wojtyla (1920–2005) studied theology and philosophy, writing a thesis on the ethics of Max Scheler at Lublin Catholic University in his native Poland and later a treatise on philosophical anthropology.

[13] Nozick (1938–2002) was Arthur Kingsley Porter Professor of Philosophy at Harvard University. He wrote on epistemology, most influentially on skepticism and fallibilism, but is perhaps best known for his defense of libertarian political theory.

or activity, but more widely in the way we function, insofar as that functioning is, or should be, responsive to reasons" (Raz 2002: 71)? Critical thinking need not involve searching for a reason upon which to hang every belief. Heidegger, for one, argues that "[t]o think critically means to distinguish constantly between that which requires proof for its justification and that which, to confirm its truth, demands simple catching sight of it and taking it in" (1976: 26; quoted in Macquarrie 1994: 103). The difference in perspective can be explained by noting that I am not attempting to explicate the means by which one takes in truth, but rather the purpose and value of basing one's commitments on reasons and (what hopefully follows) gaining the social status of entitlement to one's commitments (namely, justification).

We make public use of reason by, for example, making arguments to each other, where we draw out the consequences of commonly-shared conceptions. In this way, we may discover that we are each rationally committed to a conclusion just in virtue of commitments we already hold. However, the prospects for reasoning from commonly-shared conceptions seem dim in a pluralistic society such as ours. If your reason for opposing stem cell research stems from your religious beliefs, and I do not share your religious beliefs, you are unlikely to convince me of your conclusion by arguing on those grounds. We may be able to find common ground elsewhere among our collective commitments and pursue an answer to the ethical question on that basis. But that project might fail too. We might not share enough basic conceptions and commitments to permit either of us to justify an ethical position to the other. If that is the case, then what is the point of the public use of reason?

It would give short shrift to the edifying potential of pursuing public justification to turn away from fundamental disagreements as discursive dead ends and attend only to conceptions and commitments that are more likely to be shared and, thus, yield further agreement. One part of the edifying potential of attempting public justification is that answering the question "What reasons can I give to others to support the decisions and attitudes that I think are wise?" requires deep reflection. When we have to make a case to an adversary, we are forced to differentiate between: (a) the commitments that we need to defend so as to rationally support our view; and (b) those attachments that are not rationally implicated by the matter at hand. Scrutinizing the grounds of our own beliefs in this way not only serves the pursuit of self-knowledge; it also brings to the fore the disagreements that need to be overcome and takes off the table those differences that are immaterial to the issue at hand. Critical scrutiny involves "trying to understand the full significance of values without the hindrance of defensive reactions" (Krishnamurti 1996: 10), that is, reactions causing us to oppose a competing view rather than understand what is actually at stake in the argument.

It can also be edifying to attempt public justification, because sometimes what causes each of us to advocate certain decisions and attitudes has nothing to do with adequate rational grounds and everything to do with preconception, prejudice, habit, strategy, pride, solidarity, or concern for reputation. And even if we were to conclude that these modes of acquiring beliefs are sometimes morally and rationally permissible, none of them are strongly *veritistic*, that is, oriented primarily toward the production of true belief (see, e.g., Goldman 1999: ch. 3). If the grounds of a belief are frankly discussed, then we are more likely to discover whether it is true and correct it if it is false. If it is false, and we know how the belief was formed, we can also correct the mode that led to its formation.

The edifying potential of pursuing public justification can best be accessed precisely when the grounds of our conceptions and commitments are *least likely* to be shared by others. In these cases, there is the prospect of learning from each other, being enlightened by the interaction, over against agreeing with or refuting each other. For example, when someone justifies a position by, for example, marshaling religious reasons, it is commonplace for some to object that only secular reasons are appropriate in public deliberations. This is a mistake, as Habermas (2006: 10) has observed, in addressing the subject of public justification in politics. The liberal state, he writes:

> must not discourage religious persons and communities from also expressing themselves politically *as such* [i.e. without having to find secular correlates for religious reasons], for it cannot know whether secular society would not otherwise cut itself off from key resources for the creation of meaning and identity. Secular citizens or those of other religious persuasions can under certain circumstances learn something from religious contributions; this is, for example, the case if they recognize in the normative truth content of a religious utterance hidden intuitions of their own.

The insight applies beyond a political context. Explicating unfamiliar conceptions and offering justifications that build upon "the normative truth content" (that is, true statements on issues of value) of traditions that are not universally shared has the effect of making available to the public "resources for the creation of meaning and identity" that may help to address common problems. These resources need not be accepted on any authority, because they might be corroborated by the independent intuitions of others, which might have been present but remained inactive.

There may, thus, be tension, but not outright conflict between Habermas's view and that of John Rawls,[14] who wrote: "Our exercise of political power is proper only when we sincerely believe that the reasons we would offer for our political actions . . . are sufficient, and we also reasonably think that other citizens might also reasonably accept those reasons" (1999: 137, cf. 14). I assume that if, for example, religions reasons expressed normative truth content that others could discern and thus "reasonably accept," then the exercise of political power on the basis of religions reasons would be proper, at least from the perspective of political liberalism, because it would be based on a truth that could just as well be expressed by sufficient secular reasons. The mistake is to think that the set of reasons that citizens can accept just insofar as they are rational, what Rawls called "properly public reasons" (1999: 144), has to consist of either secular reasons or reasons people happen to accept already, prior to their potentially transformative encounter with the conceptions and justifications marshaled in support of the commitments of others. The public use of reason involves making one's commitments responsive to reason. And sometimes this responsiveness means changing one's mind.

I have made a case for recognizing a rational obligation to explicate conceptions and justifications. But a strategic case can be made out as well. Philosophers are sometimes called upon to articulate conceptions that persons of diverse perspectives might be able to converge upon *for certain purposes*. The field of human rights is a good example of

---

[14]   Rawls (1921–2002) taught at Harvard University for 40 years before his death. He is considered by many to be the most important political philosopher of the twentieth century, especially in light his seminal contributions to the political morality and the theory of political liberalism.

how creativity is essential to strategic convergence. The specifics of any given international human rights instrument are not accurate statements of any particular creed's view of the necessary prerequisites of the dignity of human beings.[15] Yet, some have been deemed to bear a close enough family resemblance to enough of the diverse views such that there are, for example, presently 170 States parties to the 1969 *International Convention on the Elimination of All Forms of Racial Discrimination* and 176 States parties to the 1979 *Convention on the Elimination of All Forms of Discrimination against Women.*[16] Developing conceptions of rights for the purposes of international politics and law is a different sort of activity than providing rational justification for a view. Articulating international norms of right – what natural law theorists would call *jus gentium*, the law of nations – requires more creativity and practical wisdom than logical deduction. However, it depends on the same sensitivity to fundamental concerns and the possibility of intersubjective agreement that philosophical inquiry generally fosters.

The lesson to learn from the fact that there are few commitments that are commonly shared in a pluralistic society is that we ought not to view philosophy simply as a constructive endeavor, building solutions to common questions on the basis of common understandings. Although philosophy studies problems and sometimes points the way towards solutions, philosophy is not primarily a mode of practical problem-solving or consensus-building. We have the democratic political process to reach decisions by agonistic deliberation and majority vote in order to solve problems under conditions of uncertainty and disagreement. We have novelists to write about ideas and institutions that make them more or less appealing and perhaps build consensus through the aesthetic cultivation of conscience (see Rorty 1989: chs 7–8).

Even more skeptical concerning the prospects for intersubjective justification through the public use of reason, philosophers (especially

[15] The human rights instruments of the United Nations may be found online at <http://www.unhchr.ch/html/intlinst.htm>.

[16] To put the numbers in context, there are currently 192 Member States of the United Nations General Assembly. See <http://www.un.org/Overview/unmember.html>.

Michel Foucault[17] and Jean-François Lyotard[18]) have argued that the contest of rival views comes to an end only through the exercise of force (Foucault 1988: 18; Lyotard 1985: 14–17 and ch. *7 passim*). Now, the pursuit of public justification through rational inquiry has sometimes been thought to be the pursuit of an *end* of discussion, explication, clarification, revision, and edification – that is to say, as a *terminus* on which the public use of reason might converge. The view of philosophy that I have presented here conceives of the purpose of rational explication differently. The view that philosophy might *facilitate* intersubjective agreement, *promote* creative thought and sensitive dialogue, and hopefully thereby *reduce* the scope of authoritarian intervention is entirely consistent with the recognition that it is beyond the competence of philosophy and philosophers to guarantee consensus on contested issues.[19]

[17] Foucault (1926–84) taught at the Collège de France and is perhaps best known for his study of *subjectivation*: the constitution of the self through the operation of social, political, religious, and historical forces upon individuals.
[18] Lyotard (1924–98) taught at the University of Paris and Emory University. Largely on account of his book, *The Postmodern Condition* (1984), he is associated with postmodernism, which he defines as "incredulity toward metanarratives" (xxiv). That is to say, the legitimating explanations that modern individuals accepted as to why, for example, scientists are not just inventing a system that facilitates the prediction and control of the physical world but rather discovering truths about reality, are viewed by adherents of postmodernism as untenable and obsolete. One of the positions often associated with postmodernism is that the values of the modern age – including universal truths, objective knowledge, rational inquiry, moral absolutes, and democratic cooperation – are mainly rationalizations of the dominating tendencies of the elite.
[19] It may surprise some to read Foucault making a complementary point: "I don't believe there can be a society without relations of power, if you understand them as means by which individuals try to conduct, to determine the behavior of others. The problem is not of trying to dissolve them in the utopia of a perfectly transparent communication, but to give one's self the rules of law, the techniques of management, and also the ethics, the *ethos*, the practice of self, which would allow these games of power to be played with a minimum of domination." (1988: 18; cf. 1984: 379).

Appendix I: Keywords Cross-Referenced to Section Numbers

References

Appiah, K.A. (1993) *In My Father's House: Africa in the Philosophy of Culture.* Oxford: Oxford University Press.

Aristotle (1984a) *On the Soul.* In Barnes (ed.) (1984), vol. 1.

Aristotle (1984b) *Metaphysics.* In Barnes (ed.) (1984), vol. 2.

Aristotle (1984c) *Nicomachean Ethics.* In Barnes (ed.) (1984), vol. 2.

Aristotle (1984d) *Rhetoric.* In Barnes (ed.) (1984) vol. 2.

Audi, R. (ed.) (1995) *The Cambridge Dictionary of Philosophy.* New York: Cambridge University Press.

Barnes, J. (ed.) (1984) *The Complete Works of Aristotle*, 2 vols. Princeton: Princeton University Press.

Bellow, S. [1964] (1996) *Herzog.* New York: Penguin Classics.

Bilgrami, A. (1995) What is a Muslim? Fundamental commitment and cultural identity. In Appiah, K.A. and Gates, H.L. (eds.), *Identities.* Chicago: University of Chicago Press, pp. 198–219.

Brandom, R. (2001) *Articulating Reasons: An Introduction to Inferentialism.* Cambridge, MA: Harvard University Press.

Brandom, R. (2004) Reason, expression, and the philosophic enterprise. In: Ragland, C.P. and Heidt, S. (eds.), *What is Philosophy?* New Haven: Yale University Press, pp. 74–95.

Brown, L. (ed.) (1993) *The New Shorter Oxford English Dictionary*, 4th edn. 2 vols. New York and Oxford: Oxford University Press.

Bush, G.W. (2001) Remarks by the President on Stem Cell Research, August 9, 2001 <http://www.whitehouse.gov/news/releases/2001/08/20010809-2.html>.

Clinton, W.J. (1999) Remarks by the President on Foreign Policy, February 26, 1999 <http://clinton4.nara.gov/WH/New/html/19990227-9743.html>.

Convention on the Elimination of All Forms of Discrimination against Women (1979) <http://www.un.org/womenwatch/daw/cedaw/cedaw.htm>.

Cooper, J. (ed.) (1997) *Plato: Complete Works*. Indianapolis: Hackett Publishing Company.

Cottingham, J., Stoothoff, R., and Murdoch, D. (eds.) (1985) *The Philosophical Writings of Descartes*, 2 vols. Cambridge: Cambridge University Press.

Craig, W. (ed.) (1998) *The Routledge Encyclopedia of Philosophy*. New York: Routledge.

Derrida, J. (1981) *Spurs: Nietzsche's Style's*, trans. B. Harlow. Chicago: University of Chicago Press.

Descartes, R. [1641] (1985) *Meditations on First Philosophy*. In Cottingham, Stoothoff, and Murdoch (eds.) (1985), vol. II.

Descartes, R. [1644] (1985) *The Principles of Philosophy*. In Cottingham, Stoothoff, and Murdoch (eds.) (1985), vol. I.

Descartes, R. [1649] (1985) *The Passions of the Soul*. In Cottingham, Stoothoff, and Murdoch (eds.) (1985), vol. I.

Dworkin, R. (1986) *Law's Empire*. Cambridge: Harvard Belknap.

Fisher, A. (2004) *The Logic of Real Arguments*. New York and Cambridge: Cambridge University Press.

Fisher, R., Ury, W., and Patton, B. (1991) *Getting to Yes*, 2nd edn. New York: Penguin Books.

Foucault, M. (1984) Politics and ethics: An interview. In Rabinow, P. (ed.), *The Foucault Reader*. New York: Pantheon.

Foucault, M. (1988) The ethic of care for the self as a practice of freedom. In Bernauer, J. and Rasmussen, D. (eds.), *The Final Foucault*. Cambridge, MA: The MIT Press, pp. 1–20.

Foucault, M. (1998) What is enlightenment? In Rabinow, P. (ed.), *Ethics: Subjectivity and Truth: Essential Works of Foucault, 1954–1984*, vol. 1. New York: The New Press, pp. 303–19.

Goldman, A. (1999) *Knowledge in a Social World*. New York: Oxford University Press.

Habermas, J. (1990) Modernity's consciousness of time and its need for self-reassurance. In *The Philosophical Discourse of Modernity*, trans. F.G. Lawrence. Cambridge, MA: The MIT Press, pp. 1–22.

Habermas, J. (2006) Religion in the public sphere. *European Journal of Philosophy* 14(1): 1–25.

Harrell, M. (2005) Grading according to a rubric. *Teaching Philosophy* 28: 3–15.

Heidegger, M. (1976) *The Piety of Thinking*, (eds.) J.G. Hart and J.C. Maraldo. Bloomington: Indiana University Press.

Horkheimer, M. and Adorno, T. [1944] (1995) *Dialectic of Enlightenment*, trans. J. Cumming. New York: Continuum.

Hume, D. [1740] (2000) *A Treatise of Human Nature*, (eds.) D.F. Norton and M.J. Norton. New York and Oxford: Oxford University Press.

In re Guardianship of Schiavo, 780 So. 2d 176 (Fla. 2d DCA 2001).

International Convention on the Elimination of All Forms of Racial Discrimination (1969) <http://www.ohchr.org/english/countries/ratification/2.htm>.

John Paul II. (1998) *Fides et Ratio* <http://www.vatican.va/edocs/ENG0216/_INDEX.HTM>.

Kant, I. [1785] (1964) *Groundwork of the Metaphysic of Morals*, trans. H.J. Patton. New York: Harper & Row.

Kant, I. (1980) *Lectures on Ethics (1775–1780)*, trans. L. Infeld. Indianapolis: Hackett Publishing.

Kant, I. [1784] (1991) An answer to the question: "What is enlightenment?". In Reiss, H. (ed.), *Political Writings*, 2nd edn. New York and Cambridge: Cambridge University Press.

Kant, I. [1788] (1993) *Critique of Practical Reason*, 3rd edn., trans. L.W. Beck. Upper Saddle River: Prentice Hall.

Korsgaard, C. (1996) *Creating the Kingdom of Ends*. Cambridge: Cambridge University Press.

Krishnamurti, J. (1996) *Total Freedom: The Essential Krishnamurti*. San Francisco: HarperCollins.

Levinger, L. (2000) The prophet Faulkner. *The Atlantic Monthly* 285(6): 76–86.

Lyotard, J.-F. (1984) *The Postmodern Condition*, trans. G. Bennington and B. Massumi. Minneapolis: University of Minnesota Press.

Lyotard, J.-F. (1985) *Just Gaming*, trans. W. Godzich. Minneapolis: University of Minnesota Press.

MacIntyre, A. (2006) The ends of life and of philosophical writing. In *The Tasks of Philosophy: Selected Essays, vol. 1*. New York and Cambridge: Cambridge University Press, pp. 125–42.

Macquarrie, J. (1994) *Heidegger and Christianity, The Hensley Henson Lectures 1993–94*. New York: Continuum Press.

Mill, J.S. [1859] (1989) *On Liberty*, (ed.) S. Collini. Cambridge: Cambridge University Press.

Miranda v. Arizona, 384 U.S. 436 (1966).

Nash, O. (1948) I never even suggested it. In Williams A.O. (ed.), *Little Treasury of American Poetry*. New York: Scribner's Sons.

Nietzsche, F. [1882] (1974) *The Gay Science*, trans. and ed. by W. Kaufmann. New York: Vintage.

Nietzsche, F. [1888] (1967) *Ecce Homo*, trans. and ed. by W. Kaufmann. New York: Vintage.

Nozick, R. (1993) *The Nature of Rationality*. Princeton: Princeton University Press.

Nuremberg Code [1947] (1949) *Trials of War Criminals before the Nuremberg Military Tribunals under Control Council Law*, vol. 2, no. 10. Washington, DC: US Government Printing Office, pp. 181–2.

Nussbaum, M.C. (1998) *Cultivating Humanity: A Classical Defense of Reform in Liberal Education*. Cambridge: Harvard University Press.

Nussbaum, M.C. (2000) *Women and Human Development*. Cambridge: Cambridge University Press.

Orwell, G. (1953) Politics and the English language. In *A Collection of Essays*, New York: Harvest Books, pp. 156–70.

Plato (1997a) *Gorgias*. In Cooper (ed.) (1997).

Plato (1997b) *Republic*. In Cooper (ed.) (1997).

Plato (1997c) *Apology*. In Cooper (ed.) (1997).

Quine, W.V. and Ullian, J. (1978) *The Web of Belief*. New York: Random House.

Rawls, J. (1999) *The Law of Peoples*. Cambridge, MA: Harvard University Press.

Raz, J. (1994) Authority, law, and morality. In *Ethics in the Public Domain*. Oxford: Clarendon, pp. 194–221.

Raz, J. (2002) Explaining normativity: On rationality and the justification of reason. In *Engaging Reason: On the Theory of Value and Action*. New York: Oxford University Press.

Rorty, R. (1989) *Contingency, Irony, and Solidarity*. Cambridge: Cambridge University Press.

Russell, B. (1905) On denoting. *Mind* 14: 479–93.

Russell, B. [1919] (1993) *Introduction to Mathematical Philosophy*. New York and London: Routledge.

Shapiro, S. (1997) *Philosophy of Mathematics: Structure and Ontology*. Oxford and New York: Oxford University Press.

Shapiro, S.J. (2002) Authority. In Coleman, J. and Shapiro, S. (eds.), *The Oxford Handbook of Jurisprudence and Philosophy of Law*. New York and Oxford: Oxford University Press, pp. 382–439.

Sheldon v. MetroGoldwyn Pictures Corp., 81 F.2d 49 (2d Cir. 1936).

Singer, P. (1993) *Practical Ethics*, 2nd edn. New York and Cambridge: Cambridge University Press.

Singer, P. (2000) *Writings on an Ethical Life*. New York: The Ecco Press.

Singer, P. (2004) *The President of Good and Evil: The Ethics of George W. Bush*. New York: Plume.

Universal Declaration of Human Rights (1948) <http://www.un.org/Overview/rights.html>.

University of Chicago Press Staff (ed.) (2003) *The Chicago Manual of Style*, 15th edn. Chicago: University of Chicago Press.

Waldron, J. (1993) A right-based critique of constitutional rights. *Oxford Journal of Legal Studies* 13(1): 18–51.

Walton, D.N. (1998) *Ad Hominem Arguments*. Tuscaloosa: University of Alabama Press.

Zalta, E.N. (ed.) (2007) *Stanford Encyclopedia of Philosophy* <http://plato.stanford.edu/>.

Index

plagiarism
  avoidance of 5, 76
  cheating 77–8
  defined 75–6
  Honor Codes 75
  online resources 68
Plato
  Apology 108
  Frede on 58n6
  Idea 66
  on Sophists 51
  using as source 53
policies, consistency 9
politics
  debate 84
  power 114
  rhetoric 7–8
postmodernism 116n18
power 114, 116n19
preconception 60–1
  see also expectations
premise
  argument 6, 16–17, 32, 35, 60–1
  conclusion 10, 18, 21–2, 25
  reasons for accepting 36
  truth of 26
prepositions 47
prima facie 46
primary sources 69, 70, 86n4
probability 17–18
proclamations 111
pronouns 40–1, 47
properties
  objects 48–9, 97
  relational 89–90
  words 48–9
proposition xxiii, 95–6, 100
punctuation 42–3

qua 47
questions 81, 83

Quine, W.V. 48–9
quotation marks, use of 49
quotations
  attribution 64–5
  editing 49–50
  and explanations of 12, 14, 63–4
  from lectures 55–6

Rachels, J. 27
rational choice 87
rationality xxiii, 7, 38
  see also reasoning
Rawls, J. 114
Raz, J. 111–12
reasoning
  building on 37
  philosophers' love of 111
  philosophical reflection 104–5
  in thesis x
reference, theory of 48
reference books 70, 86n4
references section 76
referents 54–5
relativism 91, 92, 101
religious beliefs 110, 112
research, online/library 67–9
rewriting 11–12, 14
  see also drafts
rhetoric 8, 50–2, 53–4
rights 55, 88, 115
The Routledge Encyclopedia of Philosophy 70
Russell, B. 26

sanctity of human life 9, 101
Schiavo, M. 103n6
Schiavo, T.M. 103n6
Searle, J. 13
secondary sources 7n4, 69, 70–1, 86n4

Lightning Source UK Ltd.
Milton Keynes UK
UKHW021327190320
360610UK00008B/1368